時短模試

	模試のサイズ	難度	リーディング 設定時間	開始ページ	開始音声番号
1	クオーター①	易しめ	16分	p. 2	🔊 027
2	クオーター②	易しめ	18分	p. 16	🔊 043
3	クオーター③	普通	20分	p. 32	🔊 059
4	クオーター④	普通	21分	p. 50	🔊 077
5	ハーフ①	易しめ	35分	p. 68	🔊 097
6	ハーフ②	普通	40分	p. 94	🔊 127

【準備する物】
① **本冊子**：本体から取り外しておいてください。
② **マークシート**：p. 374 ～。拡大コピーをお勧めします。
　　ダウンロードセンター（p. 10参照）にPDFを用意しました。
③ **タイマー**：リーディングセクションの設定時間を計ります。
④ **リスニングセクション音声**：入手方法はp. 10参照。

【取り組み方】
・まず、上記の6つの中からお好きな模試を選んでください。
・リスニングセクションは、無料でダウンロードできる音声（p. 10参照）を聞いて取り組みましょう。再生を開始したら、Part 4が終わるまで音声を止めないでください。
・リーディングセクションは、リスニングセクションが終わり次第、事前にそれぞれの設定時間（上記参照）にセットしたタイマーをスタートして解答を始めましょう。
・解答と解説は本体のp. 129から始まります。解答一覧が本別冊の裏表紙にあります。

注1：ディレクション（各パート冒頭の指示文）はアルクのオリジナルです。
注2：ページの関係で、Part 3、4のGO ON TO THE NEXT PAGEの回数が増えています（本番では通常、Part 3で2回、Part 4では1回）。あらかじめご了承ください。

LISTENING TEST

In this section, your ability to understand spoken English will be shown. The Listening test consists of four parts and will take approximately 13 minutes. Directions will be given for each part. By following the directions you hear, select the best possible answer and mark your answers on your answer sheet. Please refrain from writing anything in your test book.

PART 1

Directions: In this part, you will see a picture in your test book and hear four statements. After hearing each statement, select the one statement you think is the best description for the picture. Then, mark the answer on your answer sheet. You will only hear the statements one time, and they will not be printed in your test book.

Statement (B), "They're sitting side by side," best describes the picture. Therefore, you should choose answer (B) and mark it on your answer sheet.

1.

GO ON TO THE NEXT PAGE ➡

2. Mark your answer on your answer sheet.

3. Mark your answer on your answer sheet.

4. Mark your answer on your answer sheet.

5. Mark your answer on your answer sheet.

6. Mark your answer on your answer sheet.

7. Mark your answer on your answer sheet.

PART 3

Directions: In this part, you will hear conversations between two or more people. You will be asked to answer three questions about what the speakers say in each conversation. You will only hear the conversations one time, and they will not be printed in your test book. Choose the best response to each question and mark the letter (A), (B), (C), or (D) on your answer sheet.

8. Who most likely is the man?

    (A) A salesclerk
    (B) A hotel concierge
    (C) A tourist office agent
    (D) A museum employee

9. What will happen at the museum tomorrow?

    (A) Many visitors will attend.
    (B) A special event will be held.
    (C) The doors will be closed early.
    (D) Guests will be offered a discount.

10. What will the woman most likely do next?

    (A) Go to a ticket counter
    (B) Visit a Web site
    (C) Check her e-mail
    (D) Make a reservation

11. Why is the man calling?

    (A) To arrange a delivery
    (B) To respond to an alarm
    (C) To confirm an appointment
    (D) To change a schedule

12. What is the woman concerned about?

    (A) The cost of some work
    (B) The length of a process
    (C) The reason for an alarm
    (D) The difficulty of a task

13. What will Marco do tomorrow morning?

    (A) Change a light switch   (C) Call the woman
    (B) Inspect a building   (D) Upgrade a system

14. Where most likely is the conversation taking place?

    (A) At a chocolate shop
    (B) At a cosmetics store
    (C) At a spa
    (D) At a florist

15. What does the woman imply when she says, "We specialize in customized gift baskets"?

    (A) The store can provide what the man needs.
    (B) The man was given the wrong information.
    (C) The store does not stock a particular item.
    (D) The man must pay extra for a service.

16. What will the woman do next?

    (A) Check a product's availability
    (B) Ring up a purchase
    (C) Show the man some products
    (D) Let the man sample a scent

PART 4

Directions: In this part, you will hear some talks given by a single person. You will be asked to answer three questions about what the speaker says in each talk. You will only hear the talks one time, and they will not be printed in your test book. Choose the best response to each question and mark the letter (A), (B), (C), or (D) on your answer sheet.

クオーター①
易しめ

17. Who most likely is the speaker?

(A) A restaurant owner
(B) A radio announcer
(C) A city official
(D) A television host

18. What can event attendees do this weekend?

(A) Try different foods
(B) Sell household goods
(C) Watch a sporting event
(D) Learn about local farms

19. What does the speaker say about downtown?

(A) Additional buses are running.
(B) Some roads are under repair.
(C) Some routes will be blocked.
(D) Extra parking will be available.

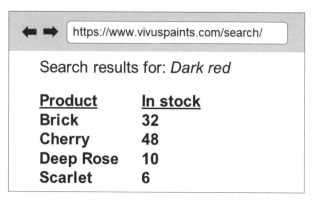

https://www.vivuspaints.com/search/

Search results for: *Dark red*

Product	In stock
Brick	32
Cherry	48
Deep Rose	10
Scarlet	6

20. Why is the speaker calling?

(A) To recommend a business
(B) To explain a problem
(C) To confirm an order
(D) To arrange a delivery

21. Look at the graphic. Which color did Mr. Stevens order?

(A) Brick
(B) Cherry
(C) Deep rose
(D) Scarlet

22. What does the speaker ask Mr. Stevens to do by Friday?

(A) Contact a product's manufacturer
(B) Make a payment
(C) Notify her of a decision
(D) Provide his billing information

This is the end of the Listening test. Turn to Part 5 in your test book.

READING TEST

In this section, you will read a variety of texts and answer several different types of reading comprehension questions. The Reading test consists of three parts and will take 18 minutes. Directions are given for each part. You are encouraged to answer as many questions as possible within the time allowed. You must mark your answers on your answer sheet. Please refrain from writing anything in your test book.

PART 5

Directions: The following sentences are incomplete. Select the most appropriate word or phrase from the choices (A), (B), (C), and (D), and mark your answer on your answer sheet.

23. The seminar attendees may leave ------- belongings in the training room during the lunch break.

(A) they
(B) their
(C) theirs
(D) them

24. Marlon Fashion's line of brightly colored jackets continues to enjoy ------- popularity among young female shoppers.

(A) clear
(B) open
(C) high
(D) close

25. It is important for managers to hold discussions with employees to set ------- goals and agree on a timeline to achieve them.

(A) specify
(B) specification
(C) specifically
(D) specific

26. Industry observers were surprised when GenTech revealed an ------- new design for its Wedge smartphone.

(A) acutely
(B) individually
(C) overly
(D) entirely

GO ON TO THE NEXT PAGE

27. Employees must shut off all computer equipment at their workstation
------- leaving the office at the end of the day.

(A) before
(B) from
(C) for
(D) until

28. The seats of Victoria Motors' Ravina minivan have been designed
with ------- in mind.

(A) comforted
(B) comfort
(C) comfortable
(D) comfortably

29. After Mr. Mattis retired, Ms. Fujii agreed to ------- the responsibility of
supervising the office's administrative staff.

(A) get into
(B) bring up
(C) take on
(D) pick out

PART 6

Directions: Some of the following sentences are incomplete. Select the most appropriate word, phrase, or sentence from the choices (A), (B), (C), and (D), and mark your answer on your answer sheet.

Questions 30-33 refer to the following e-mail.

To: rvara@cctfrance.co.fr
From: payments@workmore.com
Subject: January balance
Date: February 2
Attachment: WMOOS-00082927

Dear Raoul Vara,

Please find the ------- for your Workmore Online Office Suite attached.
30.
The monthly fee will be charged to your credit card on the due date

indicated on the document.

To view your payment history or make changes to your payment method,

sign in to your account at admin.workmore.com. -------, click the Billing
31.
menu at the top right.

-------. If you have any inquiries about your account, go to the Help page
32.
at workmore.com and select your preferred method of contacting -------.
33.

Sincerely,
The Workmore Team

---

30. (A) address
(B) invoice
(C) handbook
(D) password

31. (A) Instead
(B) However
(C) Likewise
(D) Then

32. (A) To cancel, click the link below.
(B) Refunds are processed within 24 hours.
(C) Please do not reply to this e-mail.
(D) Your subscription has expired.

33. (A) us
(B) one
(C) it
(D) you

GO ON TO THE NEXT PAGE

PART 7

Directions: In this part, you will read a selection of texts, such as advertisements, e-mails, and instant messages. Each text or set of texts is followed by several questions. Select the most appropriate answer for each question and mark the letter (A), (B), (C), or (D) on your answer sheet.

Questions 34-35 refer to the following coupon.

SAY CHEESE

984 Materson Road / www.saycheese.co.uk / 020 7315 5116

Tue. - Fri.: 10:00 A.M. to 7:00 P.M. / Sat. - Sun.: 8:00 A.M. to 6:00 P.M.

Your new neighbourhood cheese store opens on 1 October!

SPECIAL INTRODUCTORY OFFER: 20% OFF

(in-store only; minimum £25 purchase; valid until 31 October)

· Over 200 types of local and international cheeses
· Accompaniments such as cold cuts, jams, crackers, and more
· Cheese-related accessories and gift items
· Catering for private or corporate events

Ask our friendly staff for suggestions!

---

34. Why is the business offering a discount?

(A) To encourage online orders
(B) To celebrate its opening
(C) To mark its anniversary
(D) To thank its customers

35. What is suggested about Say Cheese?

(A) It only sells food products.
(B) It is open every day.
(C) It offers free shipping for orders over £25.
(D) It has helpful employees.

Questions 36-39 refer to the following notice.

Use of Locker Facilities

Lockers are available to members at no charge, on a first-come, first-served basis. — [1] —. They may be used to store clothing and personal belongings while you are training. You should not use them for any other purpose. We strongly recommend that you use a lock. — [2] —. Fitsmart is not responsible for any lost or stolen items. We also advise you not to leave any valuables in a locker, even if it is locked. Following your workout, please take your lock and the locker's contents with you.

If items are left in a locker after the facility closes for the day, Fitsmart staff will cut off the lock and remove its contents for reasons of security. — [3] —. These will be kept at the service counter for a week. If you have not claimed them by then, they may be donated to charity or discarded. — [4] —. Members will not be compensated for the loss of locks or belongings.

---

36. Where would this notice most likely be found?

(A) At a gym
(B) At an office
(C) At a station
(D) At a library

37. What is indicated about the lockers?

(A) They are available to non-members for a fee.
(B) They are monitored at all times.
(C) They are not meant for storing precious possessions.
(D) They must be reserved in advance.

38. For what purpose are users advised to go to the service counter?

(A) To pay a security deposit
(B) To report lost or stolen belongings
(C) To retrieve items removed from a locker
(D) To purchase a personal lock

39. In which of the positions marked [1], [2], [3], and [4] does the following sentence best belong?

"Users are required to provide one of their own."

(A) [1]
(B) [2]
(C) [3]
(D) [4]

Questions 40-44 refer to the following e-mail and schedule.

To: Emily Page <epage@beyrthold.com>
From: Rebecca Smith <rsmith@beyrthold.com>
Subject: Workshop at Chicago branch
Date: March 10

Emily,

I reserved a room for you at the Holiday Suites for five nights (March 17-21) for your trip to Chicago. I texted the reservation details to your phone. Please let me know if you haven't received that text.

I got a reply from Rob Coome, the training workshop organizer, confirming that, yes, you'll have access to a computer. He also wants a copy of your handouts by the end of the week because they're sending the documents to a printing company. He asked me to remind you about the reception on the last day of the workshop. All the other presenters have confirmed they will attend.

Let me know if you have any questions. Be sure to pack a warm coat—it's going to be cold in Chicago!

Rebecca

Workshop: Marketing in the Digital Age   Beyrthold Partners, Chicago Office
Presentation Schedule March 18 – 20

Monday, March 18	Tuesday, March 19	Wednesday, March 20
Jean Murphy (Boston) Current Trends in Marketing	Emily Page (Los Angeles) The Dos and Don'ts of Focus Group Research	Stephen Birch (Dallas) Storytelling: Marketing Through Narrative
George Walder (San Francisco) Consulting in the Digital Marketing Age	Sophie Colbert (Seattle) Consumer Behavior Research	Harry Grey (New York) Branding
Fran Sweet (New York) Green Marketing: Assuring Eco-Conscious Consumers	Russell Bird (Miami) The Influence of Influencers	Annalisa Kirk (Chicago) Managing Customer Relationships

40. What information did Ms. Page probably request from Mr. Coome?

(A) Whether a computer would be available to her
(B) Where she should stay during a visit
(C) What type of clothes to take on a trip
(D) When she should arrive at the workshop

41. What is most likely true about Ms. Page?

(A) She recently transferred to another office.
(B) She will lead a focus group in Chicago.
(C) She will give a presentation at an event.
(D) She will go out of town on March 10.

42. What does Mr. Coome want from Ms. Page?

(A) Reservation details for a hotel room
(B) A recommendation for a printing company
(C) Her estimated time of arrival in Chicago
(D) Training documents about a research method

43. Who will talk about the environment?

(A) Russell Bird
(B) Fran Sweet
(C) Stephen Birch
(D) Annalisa Kirk

44. What will Mr. Grey most likely do on March 20th?

(A) Go to a reception
(B) Attend an awards ceremony
(C) Stay at the Holiday Suites
(D) Give a talk on customer relationships

クォーター 易しめ ①

Stop! This is the end of the test. If you finish before time is called, you may go back to Parts 5, 6, and 7 and check your work.

LISTENING TEST

In this section, your ability to understand spoken English will be shown. The Listening test consists of four parts and will take approximately 13 minutes. Directions will be given for each part. By following the directions you hear, select the best possible answer and mark your answers on your answer sheet. Please refrain from writing anything in your test book.

PART 1

Directions: In this part, you will see a picture in your test book and hear four statements. After hearing each statement, select the one statement you think is the best description for the picture. Then, mark the answer on your answer sheet. You will only hear the statements one time, and they will not be printed in your test book.

Statement (B), "They're sitting side by side," best describes the picture. Therefore, you should choose answer (B) and mark it on your answer sheet.

1.

クオーター②　易しめ

PART 2

Directions: In this part, you will hear a question or statement. You will then hear three alternative responses to the question or statement. They will all be spoken in English. You will only hear them one time, and they will not be printed in your test book. Choose the best response to each question and mark the letter (A), (B), or (C) on your answer sheet.

2. Mark your answer on your answer sheet.

3. Mark your answer on your answer sheet.

4. Mark your answer on your answer sheet.

5. Mark your answer on your answer sheet.

6. Mark your answer on your answer sheet.

7. Mark your answer on your answer sheet.

PART 3

Directions: In this part, you will hear conversations between two or more people. You will be asked to answer three questions about what the speakers say in each conversation. You will only hear the conversations one time, and they will not be printed in your test book. Choose the best response to each question and mark the letter (A), (B), (C), or (D) on your answer sheet.

8. Where does the man work?

(A) At a repair service
(B) At a dental clinic
(C) At a hospital
(D) At a catering company

9. What does the man ask the woman?

(A) If she has an account
(B) When she discovered a problem
(C) Whether a problem is urgent
(D) How soon she can arrive

10. What will the speakers most likely do next?

(A) Select a location
(B) Schedule an interview
(C) Process a payment
(D) Confirm an appointment

11. What will happen in 15 minutes?

(A) An event will end.
(B) A colleague will arrive.
(C) A table will become available.
(D) An order will be finalized.

12. What problem do the women mention?

(A) The patio area is inconvenient.
(B) A business will close soon.
(C) The restaurant is playing loud music.
(D) A reservation date was wrong.

13. What do the women decide to do?

(A) Order takeout food
(B) Sit in the patio area
(C) Wait for a table inside
(D) Go to a different restaurant

401	Elevator	402
404		Supply closet
		403

14. What is the woman planning to attend?

(A) An art class
(B) A job interview
(C) A training activity
(D) A business meeting

15. Look at the graphic. Where should the woman go?

(A) To Room 401
(B) To Room 402
(C) To Room 403
(D) To Room 404

16. What caused a problem?

(A) The man was delayed.
(B) The woman missed a sign.
(C) The start time was changed.
(D) The elevator was out of order.

PART 4

Directions: In this part, you will hear some talks given by a single person. You will be asked to answer three questions about what the speaker says in each talk. You will only hear the talks one time, and they will not be printed in your test book. Choose the best response to each question and mark the letter (A), (B), (C), or (D) on your answer sheet.

17. What is the speaker explaining?

    (A) How to use a kitchen appliance
    (B) How to make a beverage
    (C) How to install some equipment
    (D) How to prepare a dish

18. According to the speaker, what should listeners do in advance?

    (A) Allow some equipment to dry
    (B) Wash their hands
    (C) Clean a container
    (D) Put on protective clothing

19. What does the speaker say may need to be adjusted?

    (A) The quantity of water
    (B) The cooking temperature
    (C) The refrigeration time
    (D) The drainage frequency

20. What does the speaker imply when he says, "The association considered dozens of books"?

    (A) An organization has many members.
    (B) An award is difficult to win.
    (C) A process is time-consuming.
    (D) The selection criteria are broad.

21. What did Todd Egan do last year?

    (A) He received an award.
    (B) He published several books.
    (C) He served on a committee.
    (D) He appeared in a film.

22. According to the speaker, what aspect of this year's winner was praised?

    (A) Its complex story   (C) Its interesting characters
    (B) Its unusual subject matter   (D) Its attractive design

This is the end of the Listening test. Turn to Part 5 in your test book.

READING TEST

In this section, you will read a variety of texts and answer several different types of reading comprehension questions. The Reading test consists of three parts and will take 18 minutes. Directions are given for each part. You are encouraged to answer as many questions as possible within the time allowed. You must mark your answers on your answer sheet. Please refrain from writing anything in your test book.

PART 5

Directions: The following sentences are incomplete. Select the most appropriate word or phrase from the choices (A), (B), (C), and (D), and mark your answer on your answer sheet.

23. Ms. Bain accepted a salary cut in exchange for a transfer to a small town with a lower cost ------- living.

- (A) for
- (B) to
- (C) of
- (D) with

24. Employees at Medlore, Inc., support the merger proposal ------- the company's management has promised to protect their jobs during the transition.

- (A) since
- (B) through
- (C) within
- (D) despite

25. Mr. Henderson accepted without ------- when the board asked him to lead the Vancouver office.

- (A) expenditure
- (B) hesitation
- (C) division
- (D) referral

26. After retrieving their luggage, passengers should proceed ------- to the inspection area for an interview with a customs officer.

- (A) officially
- (B) particularly
- (C) certainly
- (D) directly

27. ------- applicants who lack the required three years of managerial experience will not be contacted for an interview.

(A) Every
(B) Anyone
(C) Any
(D) Either

28. During the initial period of on-the-job training, supervisors ------- monitor new employees and correct any mistakes they see on the spot.

(A) closely
(B) closed
(C) close
(D) closeness

29. Analysts say the ------- increase in global crude oil production will keep fuel prices down for the rest of the year.

(A) liable
(B) steady
(C) concise
(D) versatile

GO ON TO THE NEXT PAGE

PART 6

Directions: Some of the following sentences are incomplete. Select the most appropriate word, phrase, or sentence from the choices (A), (B), (C), and (D), and mark your answer on your answer sheet.

Questions 30-33 refer to the following advertisement.

The International Wilderness Adventure Expo is the world's biggest trade show dedicated to wilderness travel. This year's edition ------- place **30.** from June 18 to 21 in Anchorage, Alaska. -------. They represent tour **31.** operators, travel associations, outdoor equipment companies, media, and more. These ------ will take part in talks, panels, workshops, networking, **32.** and many other activities. Covering everything from hiking to rafting to mountain climbing, all of the events will focus on the ------- of sustainable **33.** travel. Registration is open now. Visit www.iwaealaska.com to learn more.

30. (A) take
　　(B) taking
　　(C) took
　　(D) takes

31. (A) You can enjoy a wide range of outdoor activities in the area.
　　(B) Contact the organizing team for more information on travel arrangements.
　　(C) The event will bring together over 1,000 industry professionals.
　　(D) With its magnificent natural environment, it's the perfect venue.

32. (A) attendees
　　(B) trainees
　　(C) advertisers
　　(D) travelers

33. (A) edge
　　(B) theme
　　(C) amount
　　(D) distance

PART 7

Directions: In this part, you will read a selection of texts, such as advertisements, e-mails, and instant messages. Each text or set of texts is followed by several questions. Select the most appropriate answer for each question and mark the letter (A), (B), (C), or (D) on your answer sheet.

Questions 34-35 refer to the following text-message chain.

Delia Sanchez (10:49 A.M.) Mark, is everything OK? Your part of the workshop starts at 11:00.

Mark Nestor (10:50 A.M.) Yes. I'm just downstairs copying my handouts.

Delia Sanchez (10:51 A.M.) The first presenter is almost finished.

Mark Nestor (10:52 A.M.) Got it. I'll be right up.

Delia Sanchez (10:53 A.M.) I'll make some announcements to the trainees before you start. That should give you a little extra time to get set up, if you need it. Just remember the lunch break starts right at 12:30.

Mark Nestor (10:54 A.M.) OK, I'm on my way to the training room now.

34. What is Mr. Nestor doing?

(A) Printing out an announcement
(B) Making copies of the lunch menu
(C) Preparing to lead a training activity
(D) Setting up a room for a meeting

35. At 10:51 A.M., what does Ms. Sanchez imply when she writes, "The first presenter is almost finished"?

(A) An event will be over in a few minutes.
(B) She will be free to take a break shortly.
(C) A presentation was shorter than expected.
(D) Mr. Nestor should arrive as soon as possible.

GO ON TO THE NEXT PAGE

Questions 36-38 refer to the following article.

Bay City—After being canceled last year due to poor weather, the Bay City Open Water 3K Splash will be held on Sunday, August 15. The annual event raises money for Coastal Action, a Bay City-based volunteer group that works to keep the area's beaches clean. — [1] —.

Organizer Christine Mathis is excited about the return of "the Splash." — [2] —. "Almost 200 swimmers have already registered," she said, "and the number of local businesses who've agreed to be sponsors will make this the biggest event we've ever held." In addition to the swim, the event will feature music and comedy performed by local performers. — [3] —.

The 3-kilometer open water swim starts at the pier at 1:00 P.M. — [4] —. Ms. Mathis noted that some participants focus on their speed, while others see it as a personal challenge to simply complete the event, swimming at their own pace.

Swimmers and volunteers can register for the event until August 12. Registration and details for participants and sponsors can be found on the event's Web site, www.baycity.com/openwater3ksplash.

36. What is Coastal Action?

- (A) A fitness challenge
- (B) A local organization
- (C) A promotional campaign
- (D) A new business

37. What is suggested about this year's Splash?

- (A) A good turnout is anticipated.
- (B) Only local residents may take part.
- (C) It is being held for the first time.
- (D) The weather may cause problems.

38. In which of the positions marked [1], [2], [3], and [4] does the following sentence best belong?

"An outdoor stage will be set up in Waterfront Park, near the Bay City Pier."

- (A) [1]
- (B) [2]
- (C) [3]
- (D) [4]

GO ON TO THE NEXT PAGE

Questions 39-42 refer to the following memo.

MEMO

To: All Sherwood Architecture employees
From: Penny Jackson, Office Manager
Date: June 14

As previously announced, we are renovating the main reception area this summer. Clayton Enterprises has been chosen as the contractor. The work will take around two weeks, beginning on July 3. Once complete, the reception will have bigger windows and a new, more spacious layout. There will be comfortable couches and a side table with complimentary snacks and coffee for visitors.

We will also upgrade the conference rooms with new leather chairs, high-quality projection equipment, and streamlined tables. This will enable us to comfortably seat 12 people in each room. The goal is to make a better impression on visiting customers. We ask that you treat the new furnishings with care and help keep them in good condition.

While the work is in progress, you will need to enter the office via the rear and pass through the storage area. There may be some disruption during working hours due to construction noise. Please also note that the two parking spots nearest the main entrance will be reserved for Clayton Enterprises' vehicles. Thank you for your patience and understanding.

39. What is indicated about Clayton Enterprises?

(A) It will start work two weeks behind schedule.
(B) It will carry out some renovations.
(C) It is a client of Sherwood Architecture.
(D) It made an announcement on June 14.

40. According to the memo, what will NOT happen during the renovations?

(A) Some windows will be enlarged.
(B) Some furniture will be replaced.
(C) The reception area will be redesigned.
(D) A conference room will be added.

41. The word "treat" in paragraph 2, line 4, is closest in meaning to

(A) dellght
(B) give
(C) process
(D) handle

42. What does Ms. Jackson ask employees to do?

(A) Enter by a different door
(B) Park in the reserved spaces
(C) Help themselves to refreshments
(D) Keep the storage area locked

GO ON TO THE NEXT PAGE

Questions 43-47 refer to the following e-mail and Web pages.

To: Vivian Welch
From: orders@wildchildcosmetics.com
Date: October 17
Subject: Order Number 004777

Dear Vivian Welch,

Our warehouse has processed your order and shipped your items!

Product	Number	Quantity	Price
Lipstick – Nouveau Pink	NP005	3	$ 2.97
Nail Polish – French Crème	FC010	6	$ 7.74
Subtotal			$10.71
Tax			$ 0.54
Shipping			$ 4.95
Total		9	$16.20

Ship to: Vivian Welch, 377 Marianne Street, Kimberley, British Columbia
V1A 2A6 CANADA

Provider: FreightExpress   Tracking number: 10008627

Contact orders@wildchildcosmetics.com with any inquiries, taking care to include the Order Number in your message. Please understand that we do not accept returns for any reason except defective items.

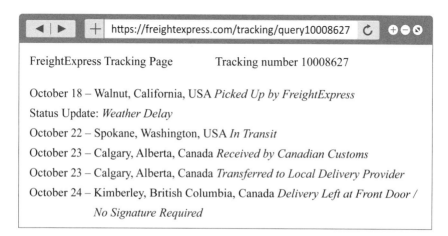

https://freightexpress.com/tracking/query10008627

FreightExpress Tracking Page   Tracking number 10008627

October 18 – Walnut, California, USA *Picked Up by FreightExpress*

Status Update: *Weather Delay*

October 22 – Spokane, Washington, USA *In Transit*

October 23 – Calgary, Alberta, Canada *Received by Canadian Customs*

October 23 – Calgary, Alberta, Canada *Transferred to Local Delivery Provider*

October 24 – Kimberley, British Columbia, Canada *Delivery Left at Front Door /*
No Signature Required

Order History   Customer: Vivian Welch

October 17   Order Number 004777 $22.34

                9 items (Click here for details)

October 26   Order Number 004777   -$2.97

                Return: 3 items (Product Number NP005) for refund

---

43. What is the purpose of the e-mail?

(A) To alert a customer to a price change
(B) To acknowledge a change to an order
(C) To confirm shipment of a purchase
(D) To answer an inquiry about a return

44. What is most likely true about Wild Child Cosmetics?

(A) It offers free shipping for orders over $20.
(B) It has a warehouse in California.
(C) It does not have any retail stores.
(D) It only ships orders domestically.

45. What is NOT indicated on the first Web page?

(A) A shipment was delayed by bad weather.
(B) A Canadian company completed a delivery.
(C) A shipment reached Canada on October 23.
(D) A delivery recipient signed for a package.

46. What is shown on the second Web page?

(A) The number of items in an order
(B) A customer's payment method
(C) The date a shipment arrived
(D) A customer's mailing address

47. Why did Ms. Welch most likely receive a partial refund on her order?

(A) It contained the wrong item.
(B) It was missing an item.
(C) It included some defective lipsticks.
(D) It arrived later than scheduled.

Stop! This is the end of the test. If you finish before time is called, you may go back to Parts 5, 6, and 7 and check your work.

31

LISTENING TEST

In this section, your ability to understand spoken English will be shown. The Listening test consists of four parts and will take approximately 14 minutes. Directions will be given for each part. By following the directions you hear, select the best possible answer and mark your answers on your answer sheet. Please refrain from writing anything in your test book.

PART 1

Directions: In this part, you will see a picture in your test book and hear four statements. After hearing each statement, select the one statement you think is the best description for the picture. Then, mark the answer on your answer sheet. You will only hear the statements one time, and they will not be printed in your test book.

Statement (B), "They're sitting side by side," best describes the picture. Therefore, you should choose answer (B) and mark it on your answer sheet.

1.

2.

GO ON TO THE NEXT PAGE ▶

PART 2

Directions: In this part, you will hear a question or statement. You will then hear three alternative responses to the question or statement. They will all be spoken in English. You will only hear them one time, and they will not be printed in your test book. Choose the best response to each question and mark the letter (A), (B), or (C) on your answer sheet.

3. Mark your answer on your answer sheet.

4. Mark your answer on your answer sheet.

5. Mark your answer on your answer sheet.

6. Mark your answer on your answer sheet.

7. Mark your answer on your answer sheet.

8. Mark your answer on your answer sheet.

PART 3

Directions: In this part, you will hear conversations between two or more people. You will be asked to answer three questions about what the speakers say in each conversation. You will only hear the conversations one time, and they will not be printed in your test book. Choose the best response to each question and mark the letter (A), (B), (C), or (D) on your answer sheet.

9. What are the speakers discussing?

(A) Contacting the head office
(B) Using a law firm's services
(C) Extending a contract
(D) Revising an agreement

10. What did the man do this morning?

(A) He reviewed a document.
(B) He prepared a new contract.
(C) He attended some meetings.
(D) He visited Staley Corporation.

11. When will a document be ready for the legal department?

(A) In the next few minutes
(B) Shortly after lunch
(C) At the end of the day
(D) Tomorrow morning

12. What is the woman doing?

(A) Arriving at an event
(B) Delivering some designs
(C) Checking in at a hotel
(D) Signing a contract

13. Why is the woman concerned?

(A) She did not pay for a room.
(B) She is not included on a list.
(C) She did not hear from her supervisor.
(D) She is late for a meeting.

14. What does the man ask the woman to do?

(A) Show some identification
(B) Go to a different room
(C) Fill out a registration form
(D) Make her own name tag

GO ON TO THE NEXT PAGE

For Sale – Acoustic Guitar

just 6 months old!

$200 – excellent condition

Pick up weekdays after 7 P.M.

100 Hendricks Avenue

15. What does the woman ask about the guitar?

(A) Its age
(B) Its color
(C) Its brand
(D) Its size

16. Why is the man selling the guitar?

(A) He does not have a place to practice.
(B) He does not play it often.
(C) He is moving because of work.
(D) He purchased a new one.

17. Look at the graphic. According to the man, which number is incorrect?

(A) 6
(B) 7
(C) 100
(D) 200

PART 4

Directions: In this part, you will hear some talks given by a single person. You will be asked to answer three questions about what the speaker says in each talk. You will only hear the talks one time, and they will not be printed in your test book. Choose the best response to each question and mark the letter (A), (B), (C), or (D) on your answer sheet.

18. What is being advertised?

    (A) A power company
    (B) A financial service
    (C) Home appliances
    (D) Office equipment

19. According to the speaker, how can listeners save money?

    (A) By switching to renewable energy
    (B) By using less electricity
    (C) By entering a discount code
    (D) By trading in an old product

20. What is the company's purpose?

    (A) To offer customers convenience
    (B) To promote innovative services
    (C) To raise environmental awareness
    (D) To provide long-lasting products

クオーター 普通 ③

21. What is RGB Associates?

(A) A food-testing laboratory
(B) An advertising agency
(C) An architecture firm
(D) A consulting company

22. What change does the speaker mention?

(A) Putting more women in advertisements
(B) Opening new restaurant branches
(C) Adding more items to a menu
(D) Making eating areas more comfortable

23. What does the speaker mean when she says, "This would be a costly move"?

(A) She wants to change a budget.
(B) She thinks prices should be lower.
(C) She believes a suggestion is bold.
(D) She disagrees with a strategy.

24. Who is the speaker calling?

(A) A construction company
(B) A building tenant
(C) A plumber
(D) A hotel guest

25. According to the speaker, what happened yesterday?

(A) The roof was repaired.
(B) Someone moved out.
(C) A reservation was canceled.
(D) There was a storm.

26. What does the speaker ask the listener to do?

(A) Submit an estimate
(B) Recommend a service
(C) Return a telephone call
(D) Pay an overdue bill

This is the end of the Listening test. Turn to Part 5 in your test book.

READING TEST

In this section, you will read a variety of texts and answer several different types of reading comprehension questions. The Reading test consists of three parts and will take 19 minutes. Directions are given for each part. You are encouraged to answer as many questions as possible within the time allowed. You must mark your answers on your answer sheet. Please refrain from writing anything in your test book.

PART 5

Directions: The following sentences are incomplete. Select the most appropriate word or phrase from the choices (A), (B), (C), and (D), and mark your answer on your answer sheet.

27. Gerard Ladino works with a number of area farmers to ------- fresh local ingredients for his restaurant.

   (A) source
   (B) derive
   (C) flow
   (D) insert

28. As there was no public transportation to Farah, Ms. Bonilla ------- for a local driver to take her to the manufacturing facility there.

   (A) arranges
   (B) arrangement
   (C) arranged
   (D) arranging

29. A wire transfer to Hartford Bank from an overseas account costs $35 and takes ------- three working days.

   (A) approximated
   (B) approximation
   (C) approximate
   (D) approximately

30. Bernard's Burgers, a chain with franchises located ------- eastern Canada, has been purchased by the Colvin Investment Group.

   (A) toward
   (B) throughout
   (C) among
   (D) aside

GO ON TO THE NEXT PAGE

31. Ms. Chen is a strict but fair manager who values attention to detail and has little ------- for carelessness.

(A) tolerate
(B) tolerant
(C) tolerantly
(D) tolerance

32. The use of electronic devices ------- cell phones and computers is not permitted during takeoff and landing.

(A) such as
(B) as if
(C) both of
(D) so that

33. Staff meetings at Arabest, Inc., are usually held online, as it is ------- for some employees to attend in person.

(A) inconvenience
(B) inconvenienced
(C) inconvenient
(D) inconveniently

34. Thanks to the tireless ------- of Ms. Bando and her team, the new software will be launched as scheduled next Friday.

(A) series
(B) roles
(C) efforts
(D) aspects

PART 6

Directions: Some of the following sentences are incomplete. Select the most appropriate word, phrase, or sentence from the choices (A), (B), (C), and (D), and mark your answer on your answer sheet.

Questions 35-38 refer to the following notice.

Dear tenants,

Axeminster Business Park is planning on ------- a new fire alarm system
                                           35.
for the entire facility. As the first step, a team of inspectors from JT

Security Consulting will conduct a fire risk assessment of the property

next week. -------. The team, who will be wearing JT Security Consulting
            36.
uniforms and photo identification badges, will be checking all of the units

------- the premises. We ask that you allow them access to your -------
37.   **38.**
and assist them with their inspection as necessary. Please do not hesitate

to contact me with any questions or concerns you may have.

Regards,

Michelle Fields

Property Manager

35. (A) install
(B) installed
(C) installing
(D) installs

36. (A) Thankfully, the damage
from the fire proved to
be minimal.
(B) The inspection will begin
at 9:00 A.M. on Tuesday.
(C) There is no need for you
to do anything during
this process.
(D) If you are interested in
the position, drop by my
office anytime.

37. (A) on
(B) at
(C) with
(D) to

38. (A) vehicles
(B) computers
(C) documents
(D) offices

GO ON TO THE NEXT PAGE

PART 7

Directions: In this part, you will read a selection of texts, such as advertisements, e-mails, and instant messages. Each text or set of texts is followed by several questions. Select the most appropriate answer for each question and mark the letter (A), (B), (C), or (D) on your answer sheet.

Questions 39-40 refer to the following text message.

RENT-N-RIDE
August 23, 9:59 A.M.

Dagmar Krawicz, thank you for reserving a car via the Rent-N-Ride online portal. Here are your booking details:

Reservation #1519510
Pick-up: Thursday, August 26, 4:00 P.M., at Lorimer Airport
Drop-off: Sunday, August 29, 4:00 P.M., at pick-up point
Vehicle: Mid-size electric car
Estimated total: $258.40
Base rate: $220.00
Discount code: N/A
Taxes & fees: $38.40

Cancellations are free up to 24 hours in advance. Otherwise, on August 26, the full amount will be charged to your credit card. To make changes or cancel, click here.

39. What is most likely true about Ms. Krawicz?

(A) She made the reservation by phone.

(B) She will benefit from a special rental rate.

(C) She must purchase gasoline before returning the car.

(D) She will leave the vehicle at Lorimer Airport.

40. According to the text message, what can Ms. Krawicz do no later than August 25?

(A) Make a free cancellation

(B) Confirm a reservation

(C) Complete a payment

(D) Change a payment method

GO ON TO THE NEXT PAGE

Questions 41-43 refer to the following e-mail.

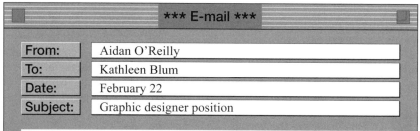

*** E-mail ***

From:	Aidan O'Reilly
To:	Kathleen Blum
Date:	February 22
Subject:	Graphic designer position

Hi Kathleen,

Per our phone conversation yesterday, I have discussed the proposed salary for the graphic designer position with my team. While we appreciate your advice, our budget is unfortunately limited. Please move forward with the hiring process based on the salary I mentioned.

As discussed, the job description should emphasize that:
- Candidates must have three years' experience, preferably in the advertising field.
- They must be thoroughly familiar with editing photos and illustrations using ImageSuite software and able to manage multiple projects with tight deadlines.

- They should be available to work overtime in the evenings or on weekends when the agency is especially busy.

If your firm has difficulty finding candidates who meet all our criteria, please let me know. While we prefer a fully qualified individual, we will consider a less experienced designer if necessary. Don't hesitate to contact me if you need any other information.

Thanks,
Aidan O'Reilly
Sunburst Advertising

41. Where does Ms. Blum most likely work?

(A) At a software developer
(B) At a recruiting firm
(C) At a market research agency
(D) At a design company

42. What does Mr. O'Reilly indicate about the job?

(A) It needs to be filled immediately.
(B) It is an executive-level position.
(C) It has a variable work schedule.
(D) It requires a background in advertising.

43. According to the e-mail, what is Sunburst Advertising willing to do?

(A) Modify the job criteria
(B) Train a new employee
(C) Offer a higher salary
(D) Revise a budget

GO ON TO THE NEXT PAGE

Questions 44-47 refer to the following online chat discussion.

●Pavel   ○Syed   ○Dani   ○Alexandra

Pavel Keretsky [11:36 A.M.] Our CEO met with our parent company this morning. He had the demo of the new Island Quest on his laptop and decided to show it to the directors.

Syed Abedin [11:37 A.M.] That's an old demo. Did they know we're still working on the graphics and gameplay?

Pavel Keretsky [11:38 A.M.] I don't know. Apparently, the directors said Sigma's Ghost Cowboys looks more realistic and exciting.

Dani MacLeod [11:39 A.M.] That's a totally different product!

Alexandra Nemoto [11:40 A.M.] Island Quest 3 will have everything the series' fans have been asking for. They aren't Sigma's target at all.

Dani MacLeod [11:41 A.M.] How soon can we put together a new playable demo? Maybe with side-by-side comparisons to the games we're actually competing with, unlike Ghost Cowboys.

Syed Abedin [11:42 A.M.] End of the week. We'll have to put off testing and updating some art until next week.

Alexandra Nemoto [11:43 A.M.] I've already made a limited gameplay mode for testing.

Pavel Keretsky [11:44 A.M.] Great. We'll show the parent company how good the new Island Quest will be.

44. What most likely is Island Quest?

    (A) A sports competition
    (B) A television show
    (C) A video game series
    (D) An animated film

45. What do the writers suggest about Sigma's product?

    (A) It is relatively inexpensive.
    (B) It surpassed its sales target.
    (C) It was recently updated.
    (D) It is not a direct competitor.

46. At 11:42 A.M., what does Mr. Abedin mean when he writes "End of the week"?

    (A) Some updates are almost complete.
    (B) Testing will start sooner than he expected.
    (C) A proposed deadline is too early.
    (D) A product can be ready to show soon.

47. What do the writers plan to do?

    (A) Announce a new promotional campaign
    (B) Demonstrate the quality of their work
    (C) Release a new product as soon as possible
    (D) Adopt some features of a rival product

クオーター
普通
③

Questions 48-52 refer to the following e-mail, text message, and Web page.

To: Davis Warner
From: Cindy Morehead
Subject: Application rating
Date: February 15

Dear Davis Warner,

Congratulations! You have been certified as a rater for Deion Industries' internship selection program. As a rater, you will assess the application forms and essays submitted online by prospective interns each year. Highly rated applicants will be forwarded to our selection committee, who will interview the most promising candidates.

You will soon receive a text message explaining how to log in to our rating system, Deion-SelectNet. Please create your account before 11:59 P.M. on February 19. We look forward to working with you!

Best regards,
Cindy Morehead
Selection Committee

Hello, Davis Warner. Use the username and temporary password below to log in to Deion-SelectNet here:

    Username: daviswarner0017
    Password: PajEkhE9

Once you log in, create a new password to activate your account. You will then be able to access applications and begin rating them. If you do not complete at least 40 reviews per week, you must attend an online review workshop. Your rater account includes a manual with complete details about this, as well as rating guidelines, security regulations, and payroll procedures.

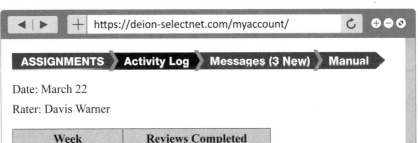

Date: March 22

Rater: Davis Warner

Week	Reviews Completed
February 22-28	51
March 1-7	55
March 8-14	38
March 15-21	50

48. What is the purpose of the e-mail?

(A) To reject an application
(B) To announce an award winner
(C) To offer employment
(D) To schedule an interview

49. What is NOT mentioned as part of the intern selection process?

(A) Uploading an application
(B) Submitting school transcripts
(C) Writing an essay
(D) Speaking with a committee

50. According to the text message, what will be available in Mr. Warner's account?

(A) Information about getting paid
(B) Links to job opportunities
(C) A complete list of raters
(D) Descriptions of new products

51. What did Mr. Warner do before February 20?

(A) He applied for an internship.
(B) He visited Deion Industries' office.
(C) He assessed some applications.
(D) He changed a password.

52. What is most likely true about Mr. Warner?

(A) He first began rating applications in March.
(B) He has not received any messages.
(C) He was given supplemental training.
(D) He underwent a telephone interview.

Stop! This is the end of the test. If you finish before time is called, you may go back to Parts 5, 6, and 7 and check your work.

49

LISTENING TEST

In this section, your ability to understand spoken English will be shown. The Listening test consists of four parts and will take approximately 17 minutes. Directions will be given for each part. By following the directions you hear, select the best possible answer and mark your answers on your answer sheet. Please refrain from writing anything in your test book.

PART 1

Directions: In this part, you will see a picture in your test book and hear four statements. After hearing each statement, select the one statement you think is the best description for the picture. Then, mark the answer on your answer sheet. You will only hear the statements one time, and they will not be printed in your test book.

Statement (B), "They're sitting side by side," best describes the picture. Therefore, you should choose answer (B) and mark it on your answer sheet.

1.

2.

GO ON TO THE NEXT PAGE ▶

PART 2

Directions: In this part, you will hear a question or statement. You will then hear three alternative responses to the question or statement. They will all be spoken in English. You will only hear them one time, and they will not be printed in your test book. Choose the best response to each question and mark the letter (A), (B), or (C) on your answer sheet.

3. Mark your answer on your answer sheet.

4. Mark your answer on your answer sheet.

5. Mark your answer on your answer sheet.

6. Mark your answer on your answer sheet.

7. Mark your answer on your answer sheet.

8. Mark your answer on your answer sheet.

9. Mark your answer on your answer sheet.

PART 3

Directions: In this part, you will hear conversations between two or more people. You will be asked to answer three questions about what the speakers say in each conversation. You will only hear the conversations one time, and they will not be printed in your test book. Choose the best response to each question and mark the letter (A), (B), (C), or (D) on your answer sheet.

10. What is the problem?

   (A) An order was incorrect.
   (B) A chair cannot be adjusted.
   (C) A desk is the wrong height.
   (D) A printer is not working.

11. What does the man say he must do?

   (A) Call a technician
   (B) Return an order
   (C) Speak to his supervisor
   (D) Sign a document

12. Why will the woman go to Evangeline's office?

   (A) To report a problem   (C) To borrow an item
   (B) To make a request   (D) To submit a form

13. What is Harriet doing?

   (A) Reporting for work
   (B) Delivering a package
   (C) Applying for a job
   (D) Placing an order

14. What problem do the speakers mention?

   (A) Business has been slow.
   (B) A process is taking a long time.
   (C) A store needs more staff.
   (D) A new worker is absent.

15. What does the man say he will do?

   (A) Interview job candidates
   (B) Switch shifts with Harriet
   (C) Take a training course
   (D) Provide help when needed

16. What does the man say about the jacket?

(A) It is the wrong size.
(B) It is defective.
(C) It was ordered online.
(D) It was delivered late.

17. What does the woman suggest?

(A) Accepting a store credit
(B) Checking the store's Web site
(C) Altering a garment
(D) Exchanging an item

18. What does the man imply when he says, "I'm on my lunch break"?

(A) He does not have much time.
(B) He has ordered some food.
(C) He will finish some work later.
(D) He is on his way to a restaurant.

GlobeRoamer.com
Rental Car Rates: Bangkok

Compact	$49 per day
Standard	$59 per day
Premium	$79 per day
Minivan	$89 per day

19. Why is the woman calling?

(A) To report a mechanical problem
(B) To inquire about a transaction
(C) To cancel a reservation
(D) To ask about a vehicle size

20. Look at the graphic. What type of car did the woman most likely rent?

(A) A compact
(B) A standard
(C) A premium
(D) A minivan

21. What does the man ask the woman to do?

(A) Send a credit card statement
(B) Provide the name of a vendor
(C) Share her current location
(D) Find a reservation code

PART 4

Directions: In this part, you will hear some talks given by a single person. You will be asked to answer three questions about what the speaker says in each talk. You will only hear the talks one time, and they will not be printed in your test book. Choose the best response to each question and mark the letter (A), (B), (C), or (D) on your answer sheet.

22. What is the restaurant celebrating?

(A) A branch opening
(B) An anniversary
(C) An award
(D) An annual event

23. What will the restaurant do this month?

(A) Hold a contest for customers
(B) Extend its opening hours
(C) Provide free appetizers
(D) Introduce new dishes

24. According to the speaker, why should listeners go to a Web site?

(A) To read some reviews
(B) To use a delivery service
(C) To sign up for an activity
(D) To make a reservation

25. Where does the speaker most likely work?

(A) At a publishing firm
(B) At an advertising agency
(C) At a financial institution
(D) At a software company

26. What does the speaker imply when he says, "That's not a lot of time"?

(A) He will request a deadline extension.
(B) A task could not be done properly.
(C) The meeting will be shorter than planned.
(D) Some work must be completed quickly.

27. What does the speaker ask listeners to do?

(A) Design a new product
(B) Take part in a focus group
(C) Suggest some changes
(D) Print a high-resolution image

GO ON TO THE NEXT PAGE

Patient : Ms. Gina Faire

Name	Morning	Midday	Night
Restatin	•		
Hydrox	•	•	•
Tropozol	•		•
Moreloc			•

28. What has Ms. Faire recently done?

    (A) She had an operation.
    (B) She underwent dental work.
    (C) She began a new diet.
    (D) She changed doctors.

29. Look at the graphic. Which medication will Ms. Faire stop taking completely?

    (A) Restatin
    (B) Hydrox
    (C) Tropozol
    (D) Moreloc

30. According to the speaker, what problem can Tropozol cause?

    (A) Headaches
    (B) Stomach pains
    (C) Sleepiness
    (D) Weight loss

This is the end of the Listening test. Turn to Part 5 in your test book.

READING TEST

In this section, you will read a variety of texts and answer several different types of reading comprehension questions. The Reading test consists of three parts and will take 19 minutes. Directions are given for each part. You are encouraged to answer as many questions as possible within the time allowed. You must mark your answers on your answer sheet. Please refrain from writing anything in your test book.

PART 5

Directions: The following sentences are incomplete. Select the most appropriate word or phrase from the choices (A), (B), (C), and (D), and mark your answer on your answer sheet.

31. Ms. Leonitis, who is based at Chronica Software's headquarters, ------- an international project team that develops new products.

(A) leads
(B) leading
(C) was led
(D) lead

32. The camera was unfortunately damaged ------- repair when it fell out of the case.

(A) over
(B) against
(C) above
(D) beyond

33. Cost is not always the most important factor to consider ------- hiring a contractor for home renovation work.

(A) to
(B) of
(C) when
(D) although

34. All visitors ------- Wildham Country Club members must check in at the reception desk in the lobby when they arrive.

(A) as though
(B) even as
(C) other than
(D) of all

35. In her speech accepting the Best New Product award, Ms. Shin
------- the hard work of the design team she led.

(A) demonstrated
(B) acknowledged
(C) declared
(D) implemented

36. Repainting floorboards is a ------- inexpensive way to give a room a
fresh new look without extensive redecoration.

(A) relatively
(B) relatives
(C) relation
(D) relative

37. With Metra Securities' streamlined application system, the -------
process of creating an investment account takes only a few minutes.

(A) slight
(B) whole
(C) faint
(D) prompt

38. Fort Walton Beach has long been known as an ------- vacation
destination for families in the Gulf Coast area.

(A) afforded
(B) affordably
(C) affordable
(D) affordability

PART 6

Directions: Some of the following sentences are incomplete. Select the most appropriate word, phrase, or sentence from the choices (A), (B), (C), and (D), and mark your answer on your answer sheet.

Questions 39-42 refer to the following information.

Thank you for purchasing the Beck Barista Pro Espresso Machine!

-------. Check the packing list on Page 2 to ensure all components and
   39.

accessories are included. Refer to the instructions carefully while -------
   40.

the unit. Follow all the steps and confirm that you have fitted the parts

together correctly prior to connecting the ------- to a power source.
   41.

Should you have any questions or concerns, please contact our customer

support team at 800-555-0215. Live chat support is available ------- via
   42.

our Web site from 8 A.M. to 5 P.M.

39. (A) Here's how to make the
       perfect cup of coffee.
   (B) We are celebrating our
       25th year in business.
   (C) Delivery is free for all
       purchases over $50.
   (D) Please read the enclosed
       manual before use.

40. (A) replacing
   (B) shipping
   (C) assembling
   (D) cleaning

41. (A) printer
   (B) unit
   (C) light
   (D) heater

42. (A) daily
   (B) certainly
   (C) finally
   (D) usually

GO ON TO THE NEXT PAGE

PART 7

Directions: In this part, you will read a selection of texts, such as advertisements, e-mails, and instant messages. Each text or set of texts is followed by several questions. Select the most appropriate answer for each question and mark the letter (A), (B), (C), or (D) on your answer sheet.

Questions 43-44 refer to the following notice.

Body In Motion is a proud participant in Williamsburg's Community Star program, which encourages residents to shop locally. The program offers $25 Community VIP Cards to shoppers, with which they are eligible for discounts at dozens of local establishments.

We are giving complimentary Community VIP Cards to all of our new and existing Body In Motion Gold Level members. Not only will Gold Members have complete access to our exercise equipment, unlimited fitness classes, and free locker rental, they will also receive discounts at Williamsburg's wonderful shops, restaurants, cafés, beauty salons, and more!

Silver and Bronze Members can purchase a Community VIP Card at our front desk. A complete list of Community Star participants is available on our Web site.

43. What is the purpose of the notice?

    (A) To provide notice of a fee change

    (B) To announce contest results

    (C) To give details about new classes

    (D) To advertise a discount scheme

44. Where would the notice be found?

    (A) At a sports stadium

    (B) At a government office

    (C) At a fitness center

    (D) At a restaurant

GO ON TO THE NEXT PAGE

Questions 45-47 refer to the following e-mail.

To:	Vera Chang <verachang@camdencafe.com>
From:	American Association of Independent Business Owners <admin@aaibo.com>
Subject:	Insurance plans for members
Date:	April 20

Dear member,

The American Association of Independent Business Owners (AAIBO) has partnered with Wisdom Solutions, one of the country's largest insurance companies, to offer special insurance plans tailored to food service providers. Wisdom Solutions' new AAIBO Group Plan is a fantastic way to safeguard your business. Available only to AAIBO members, it offers small restaurants and cafés significant improvements over other insurance providers' general liability and commercial property policies.

To learn more and enroll in the AAIBO Group Plan, simply log in to your aaibo.com account and navigate to the "Offers" page. Even if you already have an insurance policy with Wisdom Solutions, you can lower your premiums by switching to the AAIBO Group Plan. AAIBO members can switch plans with no penalty for cancellation until September 30.

Sincerely,
Claire Meadows
AAIBO Administrator

45. Who most likely is Ms. Chang?

(A) A supermarket manager
(B) A food service business owner
(C) A Wisdom Solutions customer
(D) A distributor of coffee products

46. What is the purpose of the e-mail?

(A) To respond to an insurance claim
(B) To encourage renewal of a membership
(C) To promote an exclusive offer
(D) To announce a business merger

47. What is NOT suggested as a feature of the AAIBO Group Plan?

(A) It can be cancelled at any time without a fee.
(B) It is meant to help small businesses.
(C) It was partly created for the restaurant industry.
(D) It costs less than other plans from the same provider.

GO ON TO THE NEXT PAGE ▶

Questions 48-52 refer to the following e-mail and Web page.

From: krista.emory@thestanwyckhotel.com
To: thomas.cheung@thestanwyckhotel.com
Date: March 5
Subject: Web site testimonials

Hi Tom,

I noticed that our Web site's testimonials section needs to be refreshed. One comment mentions the Azalea Theater, which closed over a year ago. And there's nothing about our new advance check-in app or expanded room service menu, which are very popular with guests.

Could you browse through some travel review Web sites to find recent comments from guests? You can pull one or two quotes from those and use them to replace older comments. As usual, please indicate the name and country of each reviewer, with a link to the full review.

Let me know if you have any questions. Thanks!

Krista Emory
Marketing Manager

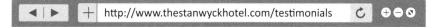

http://www.thestanwyckhotel.com/testimonials

"Even though I arrived at a busy time, I avoided waiting at the front desk thanks to the flexible check-in system. I appreciate their efforts to make guests' lives easier!" – Kai Ogawa, Japan

"Highly recommended! The Stanwyck Hotel offers great access to tourist attractions and is within walking distance of many nice stores and restaurants." – Tony Sydor, USA

"I had a wonderful stay. The rooms were clean, spacious, and well-furnished— and the rates were very reasonable for a downtown hotel. I'll be back!" – Riva Lehkonen, Finland

"The staff were so friendly and helpful. It really enhanced my visit. Special thanks to Sandy, who gave me many great recommendations nearby and provided a tourism brochure in Spanish." – Marina Mendez, Spain

48. What problem does Ms. Emory mention?

(A) She cannot find some reviews.
(B) A menu has not been updated online.
(C) Some information is out of date.
(D) A Web page has been deleted.

49. What does Ms. Emory ask Tom to do?

(A) Add links to external Web sites
(B) Give feedback about a business
(C) Send comments to her for approval
(D) Research hotels in various countries

50. In the Web page, what is NOT indicated about the Stanwyck Hotel?

(A) It is conveniently located.
(B) It is affordably priced.
(C) It was recently renovated.
(D) It has large rooms.

51. Whose comment was most likely added to the Web site recently?

(A) Kai Ogawa
(B) Tony Sydor
(C) Riva Lehkonen
(D) Marina Mendez

52. What does Ms. Mendez suggest about Sandy?

(A) She provided a ride to an attraction.
(B) She no longer works at the Stanwyck Hotel.
(C) She is fluent in multiple languages.
(D) She is knowledgeable about the local area.

クォーター④
普通

Questions **53-57** refer to the following product description, instructions, and e-mail.

Solibo Mattress Cover - $89.99

For a more luxurious sleeping experience, protect your mattress with a Solibo mattress cover made by Sleepytime! Solibo mattress covers are woven from premium fabric using 100% natural, sustainably sourced plant fibers with anti-bacterial properties.

Other benefits include:
- Multiple colors available (white, gray, burgundy, pale blue)
- Soft, pleasant texture that does not irritate skin
- Treated with non-toxic waterproofing agent to prevent spills from staining your mattress
- Two-year warranty

Caring for Sleepytime Mattress Covers

We recommend using a mattress cover to keep your Sleepytime mattress clean and extend its life. Sleepytime offers a selection of covers for all standard mattresses to suit your needs. The available options include vinyl, nylon, and fabric.

If you use a vinyl or nylon cover, you may clean it by wiping it off with a damp cloth. Never use a chemical-based cleaning agent. Wait until the cover has dried completely before replacing your bedding. Fabric covers are machine-washable. Vinyl covers may crack if exposed to excess cold or moisture. Do not store them at subfreezing temperatures or in a damp environment.

The warranty on Sleepytime mattresses does not apply to stains or damage that occur if another company's cover is used. While our covers are waterproofed, other brands' products may not be.

From: customerservice@sleepytimebedding.com   **Date**: November 7
To: robertoperez@andanohotel.com
Subject: Re: Damaged mattress

Dear Mr. Perez,

Thank you for your e-mail regarding your hotel's damaged Sleepytime mattress. Based on what you described and the accompanying photos, your situation is covered by the warranty. To obtain a replacement, e-mail a digital copy of the mattress receipt to returns@sleepytimebedding.com. Put "Claim FC213-591" as the subject and indicate the shipping destination in the e-mail. Once you obtain a confirmation e-mail, the replacement will be sent out within one to two weeks.

Please let us know if you need further assistance.

Janice Gordon / Sleepytime Bedding Customer Service

---

53. In the product description, the word "properties" in paragraph 1, line 4, is closest in meaning to

(A) belongings
(B) characteristics
(C) preferences
(D) sites

54. What is suggested about Solibo mattress covers?

(A) They only fit Sleepytime mattresses.
(B) They are made from synthetic material.
(C) They are suitable for recycling.
(D) They are safe for washing machines.

55. According to the instructions, what should owners of a vinyl cover do?

(A) Avoid exposing it to the sun
(B) Keep it in a dry location
(C) Remove stains with detergent
(D) Replace it after two years

56. What is most likely true about the damaged mattress?

(A) It included a lifetime warranty.
(B) It was protected by a Sleepytime cover.
(C) It was purchased less than two years ago.
(D) It was treated with an organic product.

57. What does Ms. Gordon ask Mr. Perez to do?

(A) Review a warranty
(B) Pay a shipping fee
(C) Mail some photos
(D) Provide an address

クォーター 普通 ④

Stop! This is the end of the test. If you finish before time is called,
you may go back to Parts 5, 6, and 7 and check your work.

67

LISTENING TEST

In this section, your ability to understand spoken English will be shown. The Listening test consists of four parts and will take approximately 24 minutes. Directions will be given for each part. By following the directions you hear, select the best possible answer and mark your answers on your answer sheet. Please refrain from writing anything in your test book.

PART 1

Directions: In this part, you will see a picture in your test book and hear four statements. After hearing each statement, select the one statement you think is the best description for the picture. Then, mark the answer on your answer sheet. You will only hear the statements one time, and they will not be printed in your test book.

Statement (B), "They're sitting side by side," best describes the picture. Therefore, you should choose answer (B) and mark it on your answer sheet.

1.

2.

ハーフ①
易しめ

GO ON TO THE NEXT PAGE ▶

3.

PART 2

Directions: In this part, you will hear a question or statement. You will then hear three alternative responses to the question or statement. They will all be spoken in English. You will only hear them one time, and they will not be printed in your test book. Choose the best response to each question and mark the letter (A), (B), or (C) on your answer sheet.

4. Mark your answer on your answer sheet.

5. Mark your answer on your answer sheet.

6. Mark your answer on your answer sheet.

7. Mark your answer on your answer sheet.

8. Mark your answer on your answer sheet.

9. Mark your answer on your answer sheet.

10. Mark your answer on your answer sheet.

11. Mark your answer on your answer sheet.

12. Mark your answer on your answer sheet.

13. Mark your answer on your answer sheet.

14. Mark your answer on your answer sheet.

15. Mark your answer on your answer sheet.

PART 3

Directions: In this part, you will hear conversations between two or more people. You will be asked to answer three questions about what the speakers say in each conversation. You will only hear the conversations one time, and they will not be printed in your test book. Choose the best response to each question and mark the letter (A), (B), (C), or (D) on your answer sheet.

16. What are the speakers discussing?

(A) A catering order
(B) A new recipe
(C) A photo shoot
(D) A Web site

17. What does the woman want to emphasize about some products?

(A) They are custom-made.
(B) They will be delivered for free.
(C) They are inexpensive.
(D) They have won awards.

18. What will the speakers do next?

(A) Greet some visitors
(B) Go to another location
(C) Modify a design
(D) Taste some food

19. What is the man doing?

(A) Signing for a delivery
(B) Mailing a package
(C) Printing a document
(D) Applying for a passport

20. What does the woman explain to the man?

(A) Where to make a payment
(B) Where to find a business
(C) How to check a schedule
(D) How to arrange a change

21. What does the man say he will do this afternoon?

(A) Drop off some documents
(B) Travel to another country
(C) Complete an online form
(D) Move into a new home

22. What does the woman say she has?

(A) An order form
(B) A menu
(C) An invitation
(D) A business card

23. Why does the woman say, "It's not a big event"?

(A) To apologize for a mistake
(B) To refuse a suggestion
(C) To correct a misunderstanding
(D) To request a discount

24. What does the man want to know?

(A) The venue's capacity
(B) The order number
(C) The payment method
(D) The event's location

25. What are the speakers mainly discussing?

(A) An internship program
(B) A new regulation
(C) A research project
(D) A promotional campaign

26. Who is the woman?

(A) A journalist
(B) A government official
(C) A student
(D) A recruiter

27. What is mentioned about the Silvera Group?

(A) It has branches in other countries.
(B) It engages in a variety of activities.
(C) It is a very large company.
(D) It specializes in technical training.

ハーフ①
易しめ

GO ON TO THE NEXT PAGE

28. Why is the woman calling?

(A) To request a refund
(B) To change an order
(C) To ask about missing items
(D) To report a printing error

29. What does the man offer to do?

(A) Make a delivery
(B) Give a discount
(C) Check a stock room
(D) Update a design

30. What does the woman tell the man?

(A) She will be out of the office.
(B) She has run out of menus.
(C) She prefers a different kind of paper.
(D) She is not in a hurry.

January 27 A.M.	
9:30 A.M.	Sylvester Wong
10:00 A.M.	Luanne Mitchell
10:30 A.M.	Omar Sutherland
11:00 A.M.	Shay McGaskill
11:30 A.M.	Dale Yamashita

31. Where does the woman most likely work?

(A) At a hair salon
(B) At a recruitment agency
(C) At a medical clinic
(D) At a dentist's office

32. Look at the graphic. Who canceled an appointment?

(A) Sylvester Wong
(B) Luanne Mitchell
(C) Omar Sutherland
(D) Shay McGaskill

33. Why does the man refuse an offer?

(A) He has a lunch appointment.
(B) A meeting time was changed.
(C) He is too busy today.
(D) A location is inconvenient.

PART 4

Directions: In this part, you will hear some talks given by a single person. You will be asked to answer three questions about what the speaker says in each talk. You will only hear the talks one time, and they will not be printed in your test book. Choose the best response to each question and mark the letter (A), (B), (C), or (D) on your answer sheet.

34. What event is the speaker discussing?

(A) An awards ceremony
(B) A film festival
(C) A concert
(D) A play

35. What can listeners do by sending a text?

(A) Vote in a poll
(B) Request a song
(C) Submit a question
(D) Win a ticket

36. Who is Pilar Sanchez?

(A) A jazz musician
(B) A film director
(C) A festival employee
(D) A music critic

37. What does Fowler's sell?

(A) Clothing
(B) Computers
(C) Furniture
(D) Appliances

38. What is scheduled to happen tomorrow?

(A) A technician will make a repair.
(B) A crew will make a delivery.
(C) Some parts will be replaced.
(D) The listener will move into a new home.

39. Why might the listener call the telephone number?

(A) To revise a schedule
(B) To return a purchased item
(C) To give directions to a driver
(D) To confirm an appointment

GO ON TO THE NEXT PAGE

40. Who most likely is Mr. Suharto?

    (A) A financial advisor
    (B) A department manager
    (C) A new employee
    (D) A job applicant

41. What does the speaker ask Mr. Suharto to do?

    (A) Send a package
    (B) Reserve a hotel room
    (C) Confirm a payment
    (D) Complete some paperwork

42. What will Mr. Suharto do on Monday?

    (A) Open a bank account
    (B) Lead a training session
    (C) Undergo an interview
    (D) Travel overseas

---

43. What is Raniya?

    (A) A cruise ship operator
    (B) An amusement park
    (C) A beach resort
    (D) A shopping center

44. According to the advertisement, why is a discount being offered?

    (A) To celebrate an anniversary
    (B) To promote a new feature
    (C) To advertise a new location
    (D) To apologize for an inconvenience

45. What does the speaker mean when she says, "Raniya has you covered"?

    (A) It provides refunds for cancellations.
    (B) It includes a relaxing option.
    (C) It offers fun activities for children.
    (D) It now accepts online orders.

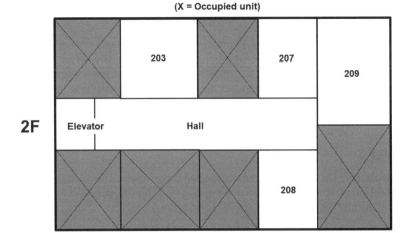

(X = Occupied unit)

2F Elevator   Hall

203   207   209   208

46. What type of property is the caller talking about?

(A) A hotel
(B) A storage facility
(C) A shopping center
(D) An apartment building

47. Look at the graphic. According to the caller, which unit did Ms. Findlay say she liked?

(A) 203
(B) 207
(C) 208
(D) 209

48. What does the caller ask Ms. Findlay to do?

(A) Wait until next week
(B) Contact a seller
(C) Indicate a preference
(D) Increase a budget

This is the end of the Listening test. Turn to Part 5 in your test book.

READING TEST

In this section, you will read a variety of texts and answer several different types of reading comprehension questions. The Reading test consists of three parts and will take 38 minutes. Directions are given for each part. You are encouraged to answer as many questions as possible within the time allowed. You must mark your answers on your answer sheet. Please refrain from writing anything in your test book.

PART 5

Directions: The following sentences are incomplete. Select the most appropriate word or phrase from the choices (A), (B), (C), and (D), and mark your answer on your answer sheet.

49. If sales remain steady, Ms. Harrington expects her IT consulting business to turn a profit ------- six months.
    (A) during
    (B) against
    (C) within
    (D) behind

50. To opt out of future messages from this advertiser, ------- click the link below and select "unsubscribe" from the menu.
    (A) simplest
    (B) simple
    (C) simplicity
    (D) simply

51. Employees who ------- to Furman Brake's new office in Eppelheim will be reimbursed for their expenses and receive a small bonus.
    (A) motivate
    (B) recruit
    (C) undergo
    (D) transfer

52. Any urgent messages for Mr. Kim between October 27 and November 2 should be directed to ------- administrative assistant, Lila Feng.
    (A) he
    (B) his
    (C) himself
    (D) him

53. Belmonte's Whisperclean dishwasher runs ------- quietly that users sometimes think they forgot to turn it on.

(A) so
(B) very
(C) such
(D) more

54. The number of students enrolled in the Blauheim School of Cooking has doubled ------- the last ten years.

(A) into
(B) even
(C) over
(D) along

55. Aviatron Research's Fly 5K is a consumer flight simulator game, ------- the company's ARFS System is a government-certified tool for pilot training.

(A) also
(B) despite
(C) whereas
(D) therefore

56. The employees at Instamart's Sattahip branch take ------- and clean the stockroom every month.

(A) inventory
(B) dimension
(C) advance
(D) exception

57. While the mechanical problem with the assembly line appears to have been fixed, the plant manager is ------- to watch the situation closely.

(A) continue
(B) continues
(C) continued
(D) continuing

58. Dauphin Island's economy has not yet ------- recovered after a destructive storm hit the area at the start of last year's tourist season.

(A) commonly
(B) fully
(C) lightly
(D) solely

GO ON TO THE NEXT PAGE

59. Viewers of the *Wyndham Times'* online photo essay may click any image to read a short ------- of the scenes and subjects it depicts.

(A) descriptively
(B) description
(C) describe
(D) descriptive

60. Ms. Martel's presentation on laboratory safety regulations was ------- and engaging for the new staff members.

(A) informative
(B) prestigious
(C) inevitable
(D) noticeable

61. Participants are encouraged to ask questions and make comments at any time ------- the workshop.

(A) along
(B) while
(C) when
(D) during

62. Ms. Tharaud will arrange training for the five new ------- starting at Calex Biofuels next month.

(A) quotas
(B) initiatives
(C) hires
(D) utensils

63. The property manager of Humboldt Apartments informs residents ------- when construction or repair work is scheduled on the premises.

(A) immediately
(B) tightly
(C) technically
(D) sharply

PART 6

Directions: Some of the following sentences are incomplete. Select the most appropriate word, phrase, or sentence from the choices (A), (B), (C), and (D), and mark your answer on your answer sheet.

Questions 64-67 refer to the following article.

The Lumberton Aquatic Complex will undergo an extensive upgrade beginning this spring. -------. These include the 50-meter swimming
          64.
pool, the smaller recreational pool, and the locker rooms. Equipment such as the diving boards and scoreboard will be replaced. The work will make the entire complex more modern and convenient for -------. The
                                                                65.
Aquatic Complex began operations almost 30 years ago. The upcoming renovations, with an estimated cost of around $12 million, will be its first major upgrade. The work ------- to take around eight months. The facility
                      66.
will therefore be closed from May through December. Some activities, such as swimming classes, will be temporarily offered ------- Merrid Pool
                                                          67.
instead.

64. (A) The work will be carried out by a local contractor.
    (B) The planned work involves improvements to various areas.
    (C) Residents are excited about the news announced today.
    (D) The facility is known for its state-of-the-art design.

65. (A) commuters
    (B) operators
    (C) users
    (D) businesses

66. (A) is scheduled
    (B) schedules
    (C) has scheduled
    (D) will schedule

67. (A) for
    (B) with
    (C) to
    (D) at

GO ON TO THE NEXT PAGE

From: customersupport@happihom.com
To: maxineorpik@ezmail.net
Date: November 6
Subject: Order #2535105

Dear Maxine Orpik,

Thank you for your e-mail. We ------- that the dish set you ordered from
68.
Happihom was cracked during shipping. Unfortunately, the product is

currently unavailable. We are therefore unable to replace the ------- item
69.
with an identical one. We have refunded the full payment amount to your

credit card.

We apologize for the inconvenience. -------. To view the selection, you
70.
may visit www.happihom.com or your nearest Happihom branch. We

hope you will find another ------- product for your home. Please contact
71.
us again if you have any questions.

Happihom Customer Support

68. (A) include
(B) regret
(C) appear
(D) obtain

69. (A) damaged
(B) incorrect
(C) missing
(D) discounted

70. (A) Maintaining the confidentiality of your data is a priority.
(B) Your credit card information has now been updated
(C) We have a wide range of other dishware products available.
(D) The delay was due to factors beyond our control.

71. (A) suits
(B) suitably
(C) suitability
(D) suitable

PART 7

Directions: In this part, you will read a selection of texts, such as advertisements, e-mails, and instant messages. Each text or set of texts is followed by several questions. Select the most appropriate answer for each question and mark the letter (A), (B), (C), or (D) on your answer sheet.

Questions 72-73 refer to the following notice.

Dear visitors,

Please note that the Addison Wing of the Warwick Museum is closed today and tomorrow while we carry out routine maintenance work and replace some exhibits with other articles from our collection. We regret any inconvenience this may cause. Other areas of the museum will be open as usual. If you are particularly interested in the Addison Wing's exhibits, please speak to a staff member at the main entrance. We will be happy to issue you a free pass for a future visit.

72. What is the purpose of the notice?

(A) To apologize for inconvenience
(B) To report that equipment is out of order
(C) To announce an emergency closure
(D) To explain the reason for a delay

73. According to the notice, why should visitors speak to a staff member?

(A) To join a guided tour of a museum
(B) To obtain free admission on another day
(C) To request access to a restricted area
(D) To have their ticket refunded

GO ON TO THE NEXT PAGE

Questions 74-75 refer to the following text-message chain.

Jana Stankiewicz   4:35 P.M.
Devon, did you leave the office?

Devon Timmons   4:38 P.M.
I had an appointment at the bank at 3:45.

Jana Stankiewicz   4:39 P.M.
Were you able to approve my purchase order before you left? I'd like to submit it tomorrow morning.

Devon Timmons   4:40 P.M.
Not yet. I'm on my way back to the office, so I'll do it later today.

Jana Stankiewicz   4:41 P.M.
Oh, I thought you were done for the day. That's fine, then.

Devon Timmons   4:42 P.M.
You can pick it up from me first thing tomorrow morning.

Jana Stankiewicz   4:42 P.M.
Thanks!

74. At 4:40 P.M., what does Mr. Timmons mean when he writes, "Not yet"?

(A) He is unable to answer a question.
(B) He is still waiting for an order.
(C) He will arrive at the bank soon.
(D) He will take an action later.

75. What will Ms. Stankiewicz most likely do tomorrow?

(A) Go to the bank
(B) Pick up an order
(C) See Mr. Timmons
(D) Leave work early

84

Questions 76-77 refer to the following e-mail.

*** E-mail ***

From:	Lisa Fitzgerald
To:	Sam Galloway
CC:	Tran Kwan, Harry Rutland, Maribel Sanchez
Date:	April 3
Subject:	Monthly all-hands meeting

Hi Sam,

At our last monthly online meeting, we noted that the next meeting is scheduled for 25 April, which is a national holiday in New Zealand and here in Australia. Have you looked into whether the Nagoya and Los Angeles teams could meet on another day? We are all available on Tuesday morning, 23 April, if that works for the other teams. We recognize that would be Monday evening for your team there in California in the United States. Please let us know.

Best regards,
Lisa Fitzgerald

76. What happened during the last meeting?

(A) A scheduling problem was found.
(B) A business trip was planned.
(C) A future meeting was postponed.
(D) An event venue was changed.

77. Where is Mr. Galloway's team located?

(A) In Australia
(B) In Japan
(C) In the United States
(D) In New Zealand

GO ON TO THE NEXT PAGE

Questions 78-80 refer to the following memo.

From: Uzma Mustafa, Accounting Manager
To: All employees
Date: March 2

Beginning on April 1, we will switch to an entirely paperless system for travel expenses. It's an app called Spendtrax, which will help us reduce unnecessary paperwork and waste each month. Accordingly, we will no longer be accepting paper claim forms.

To begin using Spendtrax, you must first set up an account. Download the app on your phone and follow the instructions. Please register using your work e-mail address to ensure Accounting receives your information. Once your account is activated, you will receive a confirmation from Spendtrax.

I encourage you to view the short introductory video on the app's Web site. This demonstrates all its basic functions. With the new system, you will upload photos of receipts instead of submitting paper copies. However, be sure to keep these as back-up until you are reimbursed for the relevant expenses.

78. Why did Ms. Mustafa send the memo?

(A) To announce a partnership
(B) To specify a deadline
(C) To introduce a new system
(D) To recommend a company

79. Why should employees use a work e-mail address when registering for Spendtrax?

(A) To keep their personal information secret
(B) To provide their company with their input
(C) To download the app on a private phone
(D) To receive a confirmation from Accounting

80. What does Ms. Mustafa advise employees to do?

(A) Back up financial data
(B) Fill out a claim form
(C) Confirm completion of a task
(D) Keep receipts

Questions 81-83 refer to the following notice.

Interruption to Water Service

On September 22, a Public Works crew will carry out scheduled work on the water main on Lofton Street. —[1]—. The work is part of Aniello City's ongoing infrastructure enhancement program. We are installing new pipes in place of aging ones nearing the end of their lifespan. —[2]—.

As a result of this work, water service to your property will be temporarily cut off from 8 A.M. to around 4 P.M. —[3]—. The crew will do its best to expedite the work, so that the service interruption will be minimized. Prior to the scheduled start time, you should store water to use during the day, if necessary.

—[4]—. Run the tap until it becomes clear before using or consuming it. Thank you for your patience and understanding. Please contact the Public Works department at (643) 555-0851 if you need further information.

---

81. What is the purpose of the scheduled work?

(A) To inspect the condition of a residence
(B) To replace old equipment
(C) To repair damaged infrastructure
(D) To prevent water contamination

82. What is indicated about the Public Works team?

(A) It will finish the work as quickly as possible.
(B) It may begin earlier than 8 A.M.
(C) It will temporarily close Lofton Street.
(D) It may cause loud noises while working.

83. In which of the positions marked [1], [2], [3], and [4] does the following sentence best belong?

"Once the service is restored, your water may look discolored."

(A) [1]
(B) [2]
(C) [3]
(D) [4]

Questions 84-87 refer to the following online chat discussion.

● Vikram Sharma   ○ Joao Rodrigues   ○ Leanne Dao

Vikram Sharma [9:28 A.M.] It's Mallory Snipe's birthday tomorrow. We should do something special for her, like take her out to lunch.

Joao Rodrigues [9:29 A.M.] For sure. She really likes that sushi place on Cypress Avenue. We should probably make a reservation, especially if there are a lot of us.

Vikram Sharma [9:29 A.M.] I'll check who wants to go, then try to book a table for noon.

Leanne Dao [9:30 A.M.] Wait a minute, guys. Mallory has a big sales presentation at 1:30 tomorrow. She told me she'll be busy preparing for that until the last minute.

Joao Rodrigues [9:31 A.M.] That's too bad. I suppose it's too late to arrange something today.

Leanne Dao [9:32 A.M.] Why don't we get together for cake and coffee later on tomorrow—say, at 4 P.M.? I'll reserve a conference room. Someone would need to get a cake from the bakery.

Vikram Sharma [9:33 A.M.] I'd be happy to.

Joao Rodrigues [9:34 A.M.] I'll send an invite to everyone. It would be nice to get her a gift, too. We could all contribute a few dollars. I'm not sure what she would like, though.

Leanne Dao [9:35 A.M.] Let me send her husband a text to see what he thinks.

84. What is suggested about Mr. Rodrigues?

(A) He discussed a lunch plan with Ms. Snipes.
(B) He is concerned about accommodating a large group.
(C) He was supposed to work on a presentation.
(D) He would prefer to change a reservation time.

85. At 9:30 A.M., what does Ms. Dao mean when she writes, "Wait a minute, guys"?

(A) She needs to look up some information.
(B) She wants to take a break.
(C) She disagrees with a proposal.
(D) She would like to postpone a decision.

86. Who will be responsible for purchasing a cake?

(A) Mr. Sharma
(B) Mr. Rodrigues
(C) Ms. Dao
(D) Ms. Snipes

87. Why will Ms. Dao contact Ms. Snipes's husband?

(A) To check Ms. Snipes's availability
(B) To get a restaurant recommendation
(C) To ask him for gift ideas
(D) To invite him to an event

GO ON TO THE NEXT PAGE

Questions **88-92** refer to the following advertisement and online review.

From Competition to Collaboration with Stella Rhys

The best negotiations are those where everyone wins. In her bestselling book *From Competition to Collaboration*, Stella Rhys outlines a successful strategy based on compromise. In this one-day training seminar, you'll learn and practice the basic principles of her approach. Those include identifying key issues, communicating your objectives, and making proposals to benefit both sides.

April 7:	11:00 A.M. – 6:00 P.M.
April 13:	10:00 A.M. – 5:00 P.M.
April 28:	9:00 A.M. – 4:00 P.M.
May 4:	10:00 A.M. – 5:00 P.M.

Stella's approach is used by hundreds of companies with remarkable results. Take her training and find out why her techniques are trusted by negotiators across the country! Each online session costs $795 (group discounts available; minimum of 6 people).

Visit www.competitiontocollaboration.com to sign up, read reviews, or discover more about Stella's qualifications.

www.competitiontocollaboration.com/reviews

Seminar: From Competition to Collaboration
Reviewed by Benjamin Motta
Rating: 4/5

I arranged for Stella to present her workshop at my company last month. She is an enthusiastic instructor who encourages active involvement. I took part with a dozen of my colleagues, so we were a pretty large group. Stella made sure everyone was able to participate, including various helpful role-play scenarios and breakout activities. Despite being seven hours long, the event went quickly. It was six o'clock before I knew it! She definitely provides value for money. I would say, though, that it was a lot of material for one day. It might be better spread out over two sessions on separate days.

88. Who is Stella Rhys?

(A) A book author
(B) A legal consultant
(C) A company founder
(D) A university professor

89. What is NOT indicated about Ms. Rhys's technique?

(A) It is described in a book.
(B) It is taught by various instructors.
(C) It is used by many businesses.
(D) It involves explaining your goals.

90. When did Mr. Motta attend the seminar?

(A) April 7
(B) April 13
(C) April 28
(D) May 4

91. What is most likely true about Mr. Motta?

(A) He was sent training materials in advance.
(B) He received a copy of Ms. Rhys's book.
(C) He obtained a discount for the training.
(D) He took Ms. Rhys's training several times.

92. What does Mr. Motta suggest about the seminar?

(A) It should be divided into two parts.
(B) It should limit the number of participants.
(C) It should include a break period.
(D) It should be less expensive.

GO ON TO THE NEXT PAGE

Questions 93-97 refer to the following advertisement, notice, and e-mail.

Greenbrook College Book Fair – May 6 to 8
Halliwell Gymnasium, 10:00 A.M. to 5:00 P.M.
Sponsored by Damiano's Pizza & Subs

Thousands of books at bargain prices! With everything from novels to textbooks to cookbooks, there's something for readers of all kinds. All proceeds will be invested in upgrading facilities on campus. Over its 14 previous editions, the fair has raised more than $200,000 to benefit students. To learn more, visit the Book Fair page at www.gbrookcollege.edu

 Volunteers Wanted!

Each year, the Greenbrook College Book Fair counts on a team of around 100 volunteers. They handle a wide range of tasks, such as picking up donations, sorting books, and preparing the venue. We need volunteers both before the event (May 3-5) and during the fair (May 6-8). If you'd like to lend a hand, please contact volunteer coordinator Keira Blair (k.blair@gbrook.edu) with your preferred dates and previous Book Fair experience, if any.

From: Keira Blair
To: Theo Kerabatsos
Date: April 16
Subject: Book Fair

Hi Theo,

Thank you very much for your e-mail. It's great that alumni like you are interested in helping with the Book Fair. I would appreciate it if you could help us with event set-up on the day before the fair starts. I will meet the volunteer team outside Halliwell Gymnasium at 9:00 A.M. to brief everyone. For directions, please consult the attached map. It should take until 3:00 or 4:00 P.M. to finish everything. You will be served a free lunch courtesy of our sponsor. I look forward to seeing you then!

Best regards,
Keira Blair

93. How will the Book Fair's profits be used?

(A) To donate funds to a charity
(B) To make improvements to a college
(C) To construct a new library wing
(D) To grant scholarships to students

94. What is indicated about Damiano's Pizza & Subs?

(A) It will supply volunteers for an event.
(B) It published a cookbook.
(C) It has a shop on a college campus.
(D) It will provide a free meal.

95. In the notice, the phrase "counts on" in paragraph 1, line 1, is closest in meaning to

(A) looks for
(B) values
(C) totals
(D) relies on

96. What is the purpose of the e-mail?

(A) To thank a donor
(B) To agree to a request
(C) To accept an offer
(D) To explain a change

97. What is most likely true about Mr. Kerabatsos?

(A) He will meet with Ms. Blair on May 6.
(B) He informed Ms. Blair about his availability.
(C) He is currently studying at college.
(D) He volunteered at last year's Book Fair.

Stop! This is the end of the test. If you finish before time is called, you may go back to Parts 5, 6, and 7 and check your work.

93

LISTENING TEST

In this section, your ability to understand spoken English will be shown. The Listening test consists of four parts and will take approximately 26 minutes. Directions will be given for each part. By following the directions you hear, select the best possible answer and mark your answers on your answer sheet. Please refrain from writing anything in your test book.

PART 1

Directions: In this part, you will see a picture in your test book and hear four statements. After hearing each statement, select the one statement you think is the best description for the picture. Then, mark the answer on your answer sheet. You will only hear the statements one time, and they will not be printed in your test book.

Statement (B), "They're sitting side by side," best describes the picture. Therefore, you should choose answer (B) and mark it on your answer sheet.

1.

2.

GO ON TO THE NEXT PAGE ➤

3.

PART 2

Directions: In this part, you will hear a question or statement. You will then hear three alternative responses to the question or statement. They will all be spoken in English. You will only hear them one time, and they will not be printed in your test book. Choose the best response to each question and mark the letter (A), (B), or (C) on your answer sheet.

4. Mark your answer on your answer sheet.

5. Mark your answer on your answer sheet.

6. Mark your answer on your answer sheet.

7. Mark your answer on your answer sheet.

8. Mark your answer on your answer sheet.

9. Mark your answer on your answer sheet.

10. Mark your answer on your answer sheet.

11. Mark your answer on your answer sheet.

12. Mark your answer on your answer sheet.

13. Mark your answer on your answer sheet.

14. Mark your answer on your answer sheet.

15. Mark your answer on your answer sheet.

16. Mark your answer on your answer sheet.

PART 3

Directions: In this part, you will hear conversations between two or more people. You will be asked to answer three questions about what the speakers say in each conversation. You will only hear the conversations one time, and they will not be printed in your test book. Choose the best response to each question and mark the letter (A), (B), (C), or (D) on your answer sheet.

17. What kind of business do the speakers work for?

(A) A real estate developer
(B) A legal firm
(C) An accounting consultancy
(D) A hotel chain

18. What does the man ask the woman to do?

(A) Summarize a meeting
(B) Make some recommendations
(C) Postpone an appointment
(D) Watch a video

19. What does the woman suggest?

(A) Meeting in her office
(B) Taking a coffee break
(C) Copying a document
(D) Reading a quarterly report

20. Why is the man calling?

(A) To approve an expense claim
(B) To request a missing document
(C) To remind Sun-yee about a deadline
(D) To explain an additional charge

21. What did the woman do on March 17?

(A) She submitted a report.
(B) She paid a monthly fee.
(C) She picked up a rental car.
(D) She purchased some gas.

22. What does the man recommend?

(A) Getting travel insurance
(B) Submitting paperwork early
(C) Obtaining a credit card
(D) Eliminating some expenses

23. What are the speakers discussing?

    (A) Rearranging an office layout
    (B) Setting up an employee
    (C) Scheduling an interview
    (D) Reviewing a hiring policy

24. What does the man mention about tablet computers?

    (A) They are preferred by new staff.
    (B) They are cheap to replace.
    (C) They rarely have technical problems.
    (D) They have improved security features.

25. What does the man plan to do?

    (A) Plan a training session
    (B) Attend a budget meeting
    (C) Speak to a colleague
    (D) Purchase a new desk

26. What does the man want to do?

    (A) Relocate his belongings
    (B) Shop for furniture
    (C) Look for a new apartment
    (D) Cancel a reservation

27. What does the man imply when he says, "That's pretty soon"?

    (A) He needs more time to make preparations.
    (B) He is pleased a job can be done so quickly.
    (C) He thought a delivery would take a long time.
    (D) He is concerned about meeting a deadline.

28. What will the woman give to the man?

    (A) An e-mail address
    (B) Directions to her office
    (C) A discount code
    (D) Access to an online form

ハーフ② 普通

GO ON TO THE NEXT PAGE

29. What most likely was the meeting about?

    (A) Resolving a technical problem
    (B) Researching the South Korean market
    (C) Implementing communications strategy
    (D) Developing new products

30. What is Victoria concerned about?

    (A) Remaining within the budget
    (B) Understanding another culture
    (C) Keeping information confidential
    (D) Meeting business targets

31. What activity is the man interested in?

    (A) Recruiting another employee
    (B) Acquiring a professional certification
    (C) Taking language classes
    (D) Requesting a transfer

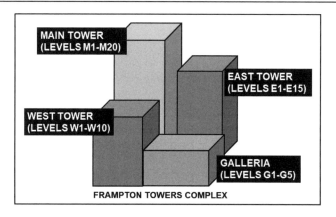

MAIN TOWER (LEVELS M1-M20)

EAST TOWER (LEVELS E1-E15)

WEST TOWER (LEVELS W1-W10)

GALLERIA (LEVELS G1-G5)

FRAMPTON TOWERS COMPLEX

32. What does the woman want to do?

    (A) Mail some documents   (C) Invite the man to lunch
    (B) Drop off some items   (D) Demonstrate a product

33. Look at the graphic. Where most likely is the woman now?

    (A) In the West Tower   (C) In Galleria
    (B) In the East Tower   (D) In the Main Tower

34. What does the man suggest?

    (A) Contacting a client
    (B) Meeting on a different day
    (C) Waiting at a restaurant
    (D) Going to another meeting place

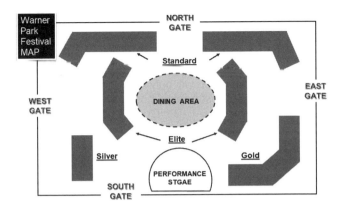

35. Who most likely is the man?

   (A) A food supplier
   (B) An event organizer
   (C) A restaurant owner
   (D) A performer

36. Look at the graphic. Which entrance will be closed to the public?

   (A) The West Gate
   (B) The South Gate
   (C) The North Gate
   (D) The East Gate

37. What does the man suggest?

   (A) Choosing a booth near the stage
   (B) Viewing the location in person
   (C) Arriving at a venue early
   (D) Making a tentative selection

Directions: In this part, you will hear some talks given by a single person. You will be asked to answer three questions about what the speaker says in each talk. You will only hear the talks one time, and they will not be printed in your test book. Choose the best response to each question and mark the letter (A), (B), (C), or (D) on your answer sheet.

38. Why does the speaker want to work with Dennis?

  (A) He offered a discounted rate.
  (B) He has worked with her company before.
  (C) He was featured in a media campaign.
  (D) He was recommended by a colleague.

39. What does the speaker want Dennis to do?

  (A) Appear in an advertisement
  (B) Apply for a job opening
  (C) Shoot some videos
  (D) Interview employees

40. What does the speaker imply when she says, "there should be more opportunities in the future"?

  (A) She expects to receive more funding.
  (B) A project could lead to additional work.
  (C) There are currently no job openings.
  (D) The company's market is expanding.

41. What does the city plan to do?

  (A) Renovate an old bridge   (C) Build a highway overpass
  (B) Improve a riverfront area   (D) Pass new laws for drivers

42. According to the broadcast, what benefit will the project have?

  (A) It will make a structure more durable.
  (B) It will add more school buses.
  (C) It will lower fuel prices.
  (D) It will introduce new ambulances.

43. What does the speaker mean when she says, "Residents will need to be patient"?

  (A) Traffic conditions will worsen.
  (B) Construction work will be noisy.
  (C) A project is behind schedule.
  (D) Fees to use a highway will go up.

44. What does the company intend to do?

- (A) Add new staff
- (B) Increase its visibility online
- (C) Move to a larger building
- (D) Target younger consumers

45. What are the listeners asked to do?

- (A) Rearrange their work stations
- (B) Review a Web site
- (C) Make time for a photo session
- (D) Meet with a new client

46. What is the speaker giving to the listeners?

- (A) A photographer's profile
- (B) A design sample
- (C) A contract
- (D) A sign-up sheet

47. Where most likely are the listeners?

- (A) At a science museum
- (B) At a botanical garden
- (C) At an airport
- (D) At a shopping mall

48. What can listeners do using an app?

- (A) Get special prices
- (B) Order food
- (C) See job opportunities
- (D) Enter a contest

49. According to the speaker, what will happen on June 2?

- (A) A site will be renovated.
- (B) A Web site will be launched.
- (C) A live performance will take place.
- (D) A video will be released.

GO ON TO THE NEXT PAGE

Orientation Schedule

9:00 A.M.	Payroll and pension plan
10:00 A.M.	IT systems
10:30 A.M.	Ethics and confidentiality
11:30 A.M.	Office tour
Noon	Lunch

50. Look at the graphic. When is the talk most likely taking place?

(A) At 9:00 A.M.
(B) At 10:00 A.M.
(C) At 10:30 A.M.
(D) At 11:00 A.M.

51. What will the speaker give to the listeners?

(A) An instruction manual
(B) An orientation package
(C) A schedule
(D) Some rules

52. What does the speaker encourage the listeners to do?

(A) Respect their colleagues
(B) Bring their lunch
(C) Keep a document
(D) Ask questions

This is the end of the Listening test. Turn to Part 5 in your test book.

READING TEST

In this section, you will read a variety of texts and answer several different types of reading comprehension questions. The Reading test consists of three parts and will take 39 minutes. Directions are given for each part. You are encouraged to answer as many questions as possible within the time allowed. You must mark your answers on your answer sheet. Please refrain from writing anything in your test book.

PART 5

Directions: The following sentences are incomplete. Select the most appropriate word or phrase from the choices (A), (B), (C), and (D), and mark your answer on your answer sheet.

53. Due to the decreasing cost of fuel, travel and transportation prices are ------- to fall slightly this summer.

(A) true
(B) equal
(C) notable
(D) likely

54. The banquet celebrating Celia Jurado's appointment as CEO of Nordberg Enterprises will be attended by the company's three ------- founders.

(A) lived
(B) living
(C) livable
(D) lives

55. Sales trainees at Brock Insurance work ------- supervision for two months before going out on sales calls unaccompanied by a manager.

(A) for
(B) under
(C) inside
(D) before

56. ------- the problems with Corinne Fashion's online shop were resolved, the company's sales began to grow again.

(A) During
(B) Until
(C) Once
(D) Given

GO ON TO THE NEXT PAGE

57. Abella Architecture has been commissioned to ------- a former retail location in downtown Nashville into the new head office of Hobart Systems.

(A) convert
(B) balance
(C) practice
(D) retain

58. Packages bearing "fragile" stickers are handled ------- by delivery personnel than items without such labels.

(A) carefully
(B) more careful
(C) more carefully
(D) most careful

59. Historian Jennifer Gupta will curate the upcoming ------- of American folk art at the Quimby Museum.

(A) version
(B) outing
(C) perspective
(D) exhibit

60. In surveys, consumers often choose ------- as the quality that is most important to them when shopping for kitchen appliances.

(A) reliable
(B) reliability
(C) reliance
(D) reliably

61. The company was originally known as Johnson Sporting Goods, but its name was ------- changed to Big J Sports.

(A) subsequently
(B) fundamentally
(C) statistically
(D) previously

62. Because the flight was canceled, the passengers ------- hotel accommodations and a meal voucher.

(A) offers
(B) offering
(C) were offered
(D) to offer

63. The Crown Hotel has renovated and enlarged its main banquet room, increasing its maximum ------- to 500 guests.

(A) capacity
(B) entirety
(C) fulfillment
(D) expectation

64. The results of the local advertisements for Lucky Candies were -------, prompting the company to expand the campaign nationally.

(A) excepting
(B) exceptional
(C) exceptionally
(D) exception

65. Clinical testing indicates that Roxena's experimental medication has ------- effects for patients with diabetes.

(A) surrounding
(B) authentic
(C) intact
(D) beneficial

66. The washing machine has a setting for bedding and a heavy-duty setting, but ------- mode may be used for blankets and quilts.

(A) both
(B) multiple
(C) either
(D) each of

67. The express train line connecting the cities of Leon and Colonia has been ------- profitable since it was opened ten years ago.

(A) readily
(B) rightfully
(C) cautiously
(D) consistently

PART 6

Directions: Some of the following sentences are incomplete. Select the most appropriate word, phrase, or sentence from the choices (A), (B), (C), and (D), and mark your answer on your answer sheet.

Questions 68-71 refer to the following advertisement.

Spirit Fashion, a clothing retailer with branches throughout the country, seeks a marketing manager. Only ------- candidates should apply. If you
68.
have held a managerial position in the fashion industry for at least seven years, we want to hear from you!

------- require a creative, motivated, and organized individual. Key
69.
responsibilities include creating original promotional campaigns and managing social media and public relations. -------. A complete job
70.
description is available on our Web site. ------- should upload their
71.
résumé at www.spiritfashion.com/jobs no later than Friday, June 5th.

68. (A) current
    (B) licensed
    (C) experienced
    (D) local

69. (A) You
    (B) We
    (C) They
    (D) It

70. (A) The marketing manager also supervises a team of five staff.
    (B) Direct any other inquiries to our communications department.
    (C) The company was founded in Brighton twenty years ago.
    (D) These duties are increasingly being outsourced to contractors.

71. (A) Recruiters
    (B) Participants
    (C) Organizers
    (D) Applicants

GO ON TO THE NEXT PAGE

Grace Sanderson
474 Trinity Street, Toronto, ON M1B 4S9

February 3

Dear Grace Sanderson,

Each year, the Pathways to Education Foundation helps millions of children access high-quality schools and learning materials. To pursue our mission, we rely on the contributions of generous donors. --------, we **72.** are writing to kindly request your support. Last year, you made a donation of $200. --------. If you wish to contribute to our --------, please send **73.** **74.** money by check in the enclosed envelope or donate online at www.pathways.org/donate/. On the Web site, you may also read further about our goals and activities. If you are able to donate, a tax receipt will be mailed to you after we -------- your donation. **75.**

Thank you for your support.

Miranda Hooper
Director, Global Education Access Foundation

72. (A) Accordingly
(B) Otherwise
(C) Nevertheless
(D) In addition

73. (A) All of them were used to directly fund our global activities.
(B) This year's deadline of February 28 is approaching.
(C) Further information about your financial status is required.
(D) We hope that you are able to consider giving a similar amount again.

74. (A) appeal
(B) situation
(C) cause
(D) matter

75. (A) will be receiving
(B) have received
(C) received
(D) receiving

PART 7

Directions: In this part, you will read a selection of texts, such as advertisements, e-mails, and instant messages. Each text or set of texts is followed by several questions. Select the most appropriate answer for each question and mark the letter (A), (B), (C), or (D) on your answer sheet.

Questions 76-77 refer to the following advertisement.

EFS, ranked the country's number one delivery company for the fifth year in a row by *Consumer Advocate* magazine, has immediate job openings for delivery drivers and warehouse staff for the upcoming holiday season. Positions are part-time and do not require previous experience. A minimum of eight weeks of work is guaranteed. Delivery driver applicants must be at least 21 years old, have a valid driver's license, and be able to lift up to 25 kilograms. Those applying for warehouse positions must be able to work nights and lift up to 25 kilograms. Applications are now being accepted at www.efs.com/joinus.

76. What is the purpose of this notice?

(A) To advertise new full-time positions
(B) To ask employees to work extra shifts
(C) To recruit temporary workers
(D) To announce an industry award

77. What is indicated about EFS?

(A) It has warehouses across the country.
(B) It has been in business for five years.
(C) It only operates during the holiday season.
(D) It has been highly rated for its service.

Questions 78-80 refer to the following letter.

Day Dental Practice
222 21st Ave., Minneapolis
612-625-9823

Emma Walker
309 19th Ave., Minneapolis,
MN 55455

Dear Ms. Walker,

This letter is to inform you that you missed your dental appointment with Dr. Judith Day at 3:00 P.M. on March 14. We have a 24-hour cancellation policy, which is stated on the consent form you signed at your initial visit.

According to our records, this is the second appointment you have missed over the last 12 months. The previous time was on November 2, after which we waived the $15 missed appointment fee. Unfortunately, we are unable to do so again. The fee will be added to your next bill and will be due at your next appointment. Please note that it is not covered by your insurance.

You are a valued patient at Day Dental Practice. Please call us to reschedule your appointment or if you have any questions regarding this letter.

Sincerely,

Lisa Dutch
Office Manager

78. According to the letter, what did Ms. Walker do?

(A) She left an item at a dentist's office.

(B) She changed a schedule on short notice.

(C) She did not show up to an appointment.

(D) She paid a bill from a dentist late.

79. What is Ms. Walker asked to do?

(A) Sign a form

(B) Mail a document

(C) Pay a penalty

(D) Waive a claim

80. What is implied about Day Dental Practice?

(A) It accepts dental insurance.

(B) It opened about one year ago.

(C) It only has one dentist on staff.

(D) It does not take cash payments.

Questions 81-84 refer to the following notice.

Attention Lake Oswego State Park visitors:

The Department of Environmental Quality has ended its water quality monitoring for the season as of September 30. Monitoring for harmful algal blooms (HABs) will restart in June next year. However, toxic algae may be present throughout the year. —[1]—. They can present serious health risks for people and pets. Before taking part in activities in and around Oregon's bodies of water, learn how to protect yourself from HABs. —[2]—.

These are caused when naturally occurring aquatic bacteria multiply rapidly in certain conditions and cover a large area of water. Some appear as a layer of green streaks or dots on the water's surface. Some look like green or blue paint floating atop a body of water. —[3]—. Others may turn the water entirely green, as if the pond or stream were filled with green paint or pea soup.

Stay safe while enjoying Oregon's lakes, ponds, rivers, and streams. —[4]—. Wash your hands with clean water and soap before eating or preparing food. Clean any fish carefully and discard internal organs before cooking. If you believe you may have discovered an HAB, contact the Department of Environmental Quality's hotline at (503) 555-0113.

---

81. According to the notice, what will happen next June?

(A) Pets will no longer be allowed to enter a park.
(B) Recreational use of Lake Oswego will be prohibited.
(C) Some park facilities will be under construction.
(D) An agency will resume checking water safety.

82. What is a purpose of the notice?

(A) To alert visitors about a paint spill in the lake
(B) To announce a change to the park's operating hours
(C) To explain how to recognize dangerous conditions
(D) To describe first-aid procedures in case of poisoning

83. Why should park visitors call a telephone number?

(A) To volunteer for cleanup activities
(B) To report finding a potential hazard
(C) To warn of unsafe fishing practices
(D) To reserve an overnight camping spot

84. In which of the positions marked [1], [2], [3], and [4] does the following sentence best belong?

"When swimming, take care not to swallow water."

(A) [1]
(B) [2]
(C) [3]
(D) [4]

GO ON TO THE NEXT PAGE

Questions 85-88 refer to the following Web page.

While counseling patients in downtown Somerset, Dr. Randal Peterson often urged them to spend more time outside. In addition to being good for one's physical health, regular walks help to improve mental health. Dr. Peterson wanted patients to experience the therapeutic benefits that exercise and fresh air could have on their mood and overall well-being.

Nine years later, Dr. Peterson moved his practice just outside of town, establishing Sunshine Counseling to add outdoor sessions to the services he offers. In these sessions, the patient and counselor stroll together through parks and rolling countryside, talking as they would in an indoor session. Patients who tend to feel awkward or uncomfortable in a typical counselor's office often find it easier to open up while walking outdoors. The patient sets the pace and can sit down and take a break at any time.

To see how counseling can benefit you, click here. Sunshine Counseling will respond within a few hours to set up a free initial online assessment, where you and Dr. Peterson can meet and decide the type of therapy that would be best for you.

85. What is the purpose of the Web page?

(A) To announce an upcoming anniversary
(B) To describe the benefits of a service
(C) To list a therapist's qualifications
(D) To give advice about selecting a counselor

86. What is indicated about Dr. Peterson?

(A) He moved to Somerset nine years ago.
(B) He runs Sunshine Counseling from his home.
(C) He manages offices in multiple locations.
(D) He relocated his place of business.

87. The phrase "open up" in paragraph 2, line 6, is closest in meaning to

(A) become wider
(B) extend toward
(C) talk freely
(D) begin operating

88. What is suggested about Sunshine Counseling?

(A) It does not offer indoor counseling sessions.
(B) It provides the first meeting at no charge.
(C) It allows patients to reschedule sessions easily.
(D) It is not currently accepting new patients.

GO ON TO THE NEXT PAGE

Questions 89-93 refer to the following text message and Web page.

Rachel Burton

Sarah Yamada (May 5, 2:58 P.M.)

Rachel, here's the itinerary for your flight to London for this year's International Hospitality Association Expo. You'll leave from Lintonville Municipal Airport at 7:55 A.M. on Saturday, June 16. The flight connects through Boston to London Heathrow and returns via the same route, arriving at 10:00 P.M. on Sunday, June 24. Note that you're using Lintonville Municipal Airport, not Lintonville Regional Airport! There's no shuttle service between them, and if you accidentally go to the wrong airport, you'll never get to the right one in time for your flight.

I'll forward your check-in credentials for the expo and hotel details as soon as I get them. Let me know if you have any questions.

[Rachel_Burton_itinerary.file]

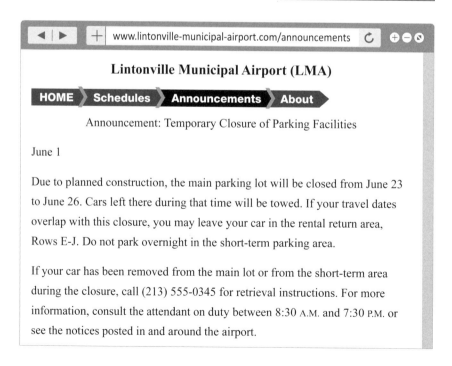

www.lintonville-municipal-airport.com/announcements

Lintonville Municipal Airport (LMA)

HOME Schedules **Announcements** About

Announcement: Temporary Closure of Parking Facilities

June 1

Due to planned construction, the main parking lot will be closed from June 23 to June 26. Cars left there during that time will be towed. If your travel dates overlap with this closure, you may leave your car in the rental return area, Rows E-J. Do not park overnight in the short-term parking area.

If your car has been removed from the main lot or from the short-term area during the closure, call (213) 555-0345 for retrieval instructions. For more information, consult the attendant on duty between 8:30 A.M. and 7:30 P.M. or see the notices posted in and around the airport.

89. What did Ms. Yamada send with her message?

    (A) An event program
    (B) Hotel information
    (C) An airline travel schedule
    (D) An expo entry pass

90. What is indicated about Ms. Burton?

    (A) She plans to attend an industry event.
    (B) She travels to London every year.
    (C) She works in the healthcare field.
    (D) She requested a later flight.

91. According to the text message, why should Ms. Burton be careful?

    (A) Tickets for the airport shuttle bus service may be sold out.
    (B) She will use two different airlines for her trip.
    (C) The connection time in Boston is short.
    (D) An area has more than one airport.

92. Why should someone call the telephone number indicated on the Web page?

    (A) To purchase a parking permit
    (B) To find a relocated vehicle
    (C) To ask about missing luggage
    (D) To get directions to an airport

93. What should Ms. Burton do if she drives her car to the airport?

    (A) Park in the rental return area
    (B) Use the shuttle bus service
    (C) Confer with an attendant
    (D) Leave it in the short-term area

GO ON TO THE NEXT PAGE

Questions 94-98 refer to the following advertisement, e-mail, and letter.

Wanted: Receptionist for Accounting Office

Schneider & McQuarrie seeks a receptionist with strong interpersonal skills for our busy office. Working closely with other team members, the receptionist plays a key role in ensuring the office runs smoothly. Tasks include welcoming visitors, answering phone calls, and handling print and e-mail correspondence. The receptionist must also manage office supplies and purchase new ones as needed.

This is a full-time position with competitive salary and benefits. To apply, please e-mail a résumé, brief introduction, and signed letter of reference in PDF format to hiring@schneidermcquarrie.com. No phone calls or in-person applications.

From: isabellemeade@abcmail.com
To: hiring@schneidermcquarrie.com
Date: March 26
Subject: Receptionist position
Attachment: 📎IMresume.file, 📎IMref.file

Dear Sir or Madam,

I am writing with regard to the opening at your firm. I am an experienced receptionist who has worked full time for a variety of employers in different fields, including a dental clinic, PR agency and, at present, a law firm. With my strong organizational skills and ability to build positive professional relationships, I believe I would be a valuable asset to Schneider & McQuarrie.

Please find attached my résumé and letter of reference. I look forward to discussing this opportunity with you further.

Sincerely,

Isabelle Meade

March 4

To whom it may concern:

Isabelle Meade has been an employee of Fitzroy & Partners for the past two years. During this time, she has proven herself extremely competent and reliable. Her cheerful attitude and work ethic make her an ideal receptionist. It is a pleasure to recommend her. We will be sorry to see her leave, but we understand her desire to work closer to home.

Please contact me at (604) 555-0338 if you need any more information.

Sincerely,

Andrew Fitzroy

94. According to the advertisement, what is NOT one of the receptionist's duties?

(A) Taking care of mail
(B) Ordering materials
(C) Setting up appointments
(D) Collaborating with other staff

95. What are job applicants asked to do?

(A) Indicate their accounting knowledge
(B) Fill out an application form
(C) Specify their salary expectations
(D) Submit documents by e-mail only

96. Which job requirement does Ms. Meade mention in her e-mail?

(A) Professional qualifications
(B) Full-time availability
(C) Interpersonal skills
(D) Ability to managing office supplies

97. According to the letter, what is most likely true about Ms. Meade?

(A) She left her position on March 4.
(B) She prefers to work at a small firm.
(C) She is changing jobs for personal reasons.
(D) She is moving to a different city.

98. Who most likely is Mr. Fitzroy?

(A) A lawyer
(B) A public relations specialist
(C) An accountant
(D) A human resources manager

GO ON TO THE NEXT PAGE

Questions 99-103 refer to the following Web page, estimate, and text message.

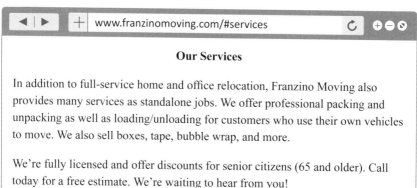

Our Services

In addition to full-service home and office relocation, Franzino Moving also provides many services as standalone jobs. We offer professional packing and unpacking as well as loading/unloading for customers who use their own vehicles to move. We also sell boxes, tape, bubble wrap, and more.

We're fully licensed and offer discounts for senior citizens (65 and older). Call today for a free estimate. We're waiting to hear from you!

Franzino Moving, Inc.

4086 West Plaza

Atlanta, Georgia

Client: Elizabeth Martinez   **Estimate date:** May 1

Move date: Saturday, May 27 – Sunday, May 28
From: 4005 Almond Court, Marietta, Georgia
To: 907B Vernon Street, Fernandina Beach, Florida
Move type: Residential, 377 miles
Estimated volume: 687 cubic feet @ $3.75

Basic estimated price:	$2,576.25
Senior Discount:	–$257.63
Other services:	$0.00 (None)
Total estimate:	$2,318.62

Note: $463.72 deposit (paid by credit card on May 1) will be applied to final bill.

The estimate provided is based on the stated inventory and conditions. Changing locations, increasing or decreasing inventory, and other variables will affect the total time and cost of your move.

Prepared by Kayla Todd

Kayla Todd
May 29, 10:55 A.M.

Hello, it's Elizabeth Martinez. I'm sorry I missed your call. I got the new estimate you e-mailed yesterday and everything looks fine. Thanks again for accommodating me after my original flight from Georgia was canceled.

I just landed in Florida and should be at the apartment when the truck arrives, but just in case I'm delayed again, I've called ahead and asked the apartment manager to let the crew begin unloading as soon as they get there.

99. What service is NOT offered by Franzino Moving?

(A) Sales of moving supplies
(B) Renting out moving vehicles
(C) Preparing belongings for moving
(D) Putting items into vehicles

100. In the estimate, the phrase "deposit" in Note, line 1, is closest in meaning to

(A) accumulation
(B) deduction
(C) payment
(D) savings

101. What is most likely true about Ms. Martinez?

(A) She is relocating her business.
(B) She paid her entire bill in advance.
(C) She plans to pay her bill in cash.
(D) She is at least 65 years old.

102. What is a purpose of Ms. Martinez's text?

(A) To inform the moving company of a delay
(B) To confirm that a building can be accessed
(C) To ask Ms. Todd to prepare a new estimate
(D) To provide directions for a moving crew

103. What aspect of the move changed after May 1?

(A) The load size
(B) The destination address
(C) The departure location
(D) The arrival date

Stop! This is the end of the test. If you finish before time is called, you may go back to Parts 5, 6, and 7 and check your work.

123

時短模試 クオーター①② 解答一覧

左から問題番号、正解、解答・解説の先頭ページを示しています。

時短模試クオーター①				時短模試クオーター②		
問題番号	正解	解説ページ		問題番号	正解	解説ページ
1	D	130		1	B	156
2	C	131		2	C	157
3	B			3	B	
4	A	132		4	C	158
5	A			5	C	
6	C	133		6	A	159
7	C			7	B	
8	D	134		8	B	160
9	A			9	C	
10	B			10	D	
11	C	136		11	C	162
12	B			12	A	
13	D			13	D	
14	B	138		14	C	164
15	A			15	D	
16	C			16	B	
17	D	140		17	D	166
18	A			18	C	
19	C			19	A	
20	B	142		20	B	168
21	D			21	A	
22	C			22	C	
23	B	144		23	C	170
24	C			24	A	
25	D			25	B	
26	D	145		26	D	171
27	A			27	C	
28	B	146		28	A	172
29	C			29	B	
30	B	147		30	D	173
31	D			31	C	
32	C			32	A	
33	A			33	B	
34	B	149		34	C	175
35	D			35	D	
36	A	150		36	B	176
37	C			37	A	
38	C			38	C	
39	B			39	B	178
40	A	152		40	D	
41	C			41	D	
42	D			42	A	
43	B			43	C	180
44	A			44	B	
				45	D	
				46	A	
				47	C	

時短模試 クオーター③④ 解答一覧

左から問題番号、正解、解答・解説の先頭ページを示しています。

時短模試 ハーフ① 解答一覧

左から問題番号、正解、解答・解説の先頭ページを示しています。

問題番号	正解	解説ページ
1	D	252
2	A	
3	D	253
4	A	254
5	B	
6	A	255
7	C	
8	B	256
9	C	
10	C	257
11	B	
12	A	258
13	A	
14	C	259
15	A	
16	D	260
17	A	
18	C	
19	B	262
20	D	
21	C	
22	B	264
23	B	
24	D	
25	A	266
26	C	
27	B	
28	C	268
29	A	
30	D	
31	D	270
32	A	
33	A	
34	C	272
35	D	
36	C	
37	D	274
38	B	
39	A	
40	C	276
41	D	
42	A	
43	B	278
44	A	
45	B	
46	D	280
47	D	
48	C	

問題番号	正解	解説ページ
49	C	282
50	D	
51	D	
52	B	283
53	A	
54	C	
55	C	284
56	A	
57	D	
58	B	285
59	B	
60	A	
61	D	286
62	C	
63	A	
64	B	287
65	C	
66	A	
67	D	
68	B	289
69	A	
70	C	
71	D	
72	A	291
73	B	
74	D	292
75	C	
76	A	294
77	C	
78	C	
79	B	296
80	D	
81	B	298
82	A	
83	D	
84	B	300
85	C	
86	A	
87	C	
88	A	303
89	B	
90	A	
91	C	
92	A	
93	B	306
94	D	
95	D	
96	C	
97	B	

時短模試 ハーフ② 解答一覧

左から問題番号、正解、解答・解説の先頭ページを示しています。

問題番号	正解	解説ページ	問題番号	正解	解説ページ
1	D	310	53	D	344
2	C		54	B	
3	B	311	55	B	
4	A	312	56	C	345
5	B		57	A	
6	B	313	58	C	346
7	C		59	D	
8	B	314	60	B	
9	C		61	A	347
10	B	315	62	C	
11	C		63	A	348
12	B	316	64	B	
13	A		65	D	
14	C	317	66	C	349
15	A		67	D	
16	B	318	68	C	350
17	D	319	69	B	
18	A		70	A	
19	C		71	D	
20	B	321	72	A	352
21	D		73	D	
22	C		74	C	
23	B	324	75	B	
24	A		76	C	354
25	C		77	D	
26	A	326	78	C	356
27	B		79	C	
28	D		80	A	
29	D	328	81	D	358
30	C		82	C	
31	C		83	B	
32	B	330	84	D	
33	A		85	B	360
34	D		86	D	
35	B	332	87	C	
36	C		88	B	
37	D		89	C	362
38	D	334	90	A	
39	C		91	D	
40	B		92	B	
41	A	336	93	A	
42	A		94	C	365
43	A		95	D	
44	B	338	96	C	
45	C		97	C	
46	D		98	A	
47	D	340	99	B	368
48	A		100	C	
49	C		101	D	
50	C	342	102	B	
51	D		103	D	
52	D				

ダウンロード特典　完全模試（200問）　解答一覧

左から問題番号、正解、解答・解説の先頭ページを示しています。

問題番号	正解	解説ページ
Part1　1	D	252
2	D	310
3	A	252
4	C	310
5	D	253
6	B	311
Part2　7	C	259
8	A	254
9	C	255
10	A	255
11	C	256
12	B	256
13	B	254
14	C	257
15	A	258
16	B	257
17	A	258
18	A	259
19	B	312
20	A	312
21	C	314
22	C	313
23	B	313
24	B	315
25	D	314
26	A	315
27	C	317
28	A	316
29	B	316
30	B	318
31	A	317
Part3　32	D	
33	A	260
34	C	
35	B	
36	D	262
37	C	
38	D	
39	A	319
40	C	
41	B	
42	B	264
43	D	
44	B	
45	D	321
46	C	
47	A	
48	C	266
49	B	

問題番号	正解	解説ページ
50	C	
51	A	268
52	D	
53	B	
54	A	324
55	C	
56	A	
57	B	326
58	D	
59	D	
60	C	328
61	C	
62	D	
63	A	270
64	A	
65	B	
66	A	330
67	D	
68	B	
69	C	332
70	D	
Part4　71	C	
72	D	272
73	C	
74	D	
75	C	334
76	B	
77	D	
78	B	274
79	A	
80	C	
81	D	276
82	A	
83	B	
84	A	278
85	B	
86	A	
87	A	336
88	A	
89	B	
90	C	338
91	D	
92	D	
93	A	340
94	C	
95	D	
96	D	280
97	C	
98	C	
99	D	342
100	D	

問題番号	正解	解説ページ
Part5　101	B	285
102	C	345
103	C	283
104	B	346
105	D	282
106	D	282
107	C	347
108	C	282
109	D	344
110	B	283
111	C	349
112	A	284
113	D	283
114	A	345
115	B	285
116	C	286
117	B	344
118	D	284
119	D	346
120	B	348
121	A	286
122	A	348
123	C	284
124	A	285
125	C	346
126	D	348
127	D	349
128	B	344
129	D	286
130	A	347
Part6　131	C	
132	B	350
133	A	
134	D	
135	B	
136	C	287
137	A	
138	D	
139	A	
140	D	352
141	A	
142	B	
143	B	
144	A	289
145	C	
146	D	

問題番号	正解	解説ページ
Part7　147	A	294
148	C	
149	A	291
150	B	
151	D	292
152	C	
153	C	
154	C	356
155	A	
156	B	
157	A	298
158	D	
159	C	354
160	D	
161	C	
162	B	296
163	D	
164	D	
165	C	358
166	B	
167	D	
168	B	
169	C	300
170	A	
171	C	
172	B	
173	D	360
174	C	
175	B	
176	A	
177	B	
178	A	303
179	C	
180	A	
181	C	
182	A	
183	D	362
184	B	
185	A	
186	B	
187	D	
188	D	306
189	C	
190	B	
191	B	
192	C	
193	D	368
194	B	
195	D	
196	C	
197	D	
198	C	365
199	C	
200	A	